QUILT

STEP BY STEP

QUILT
STEP BY STEP

PATCHWORK AND APPLIQUÉ • TECHNIQUES, DESIGNS, AND PROJECTS

CONTENTS

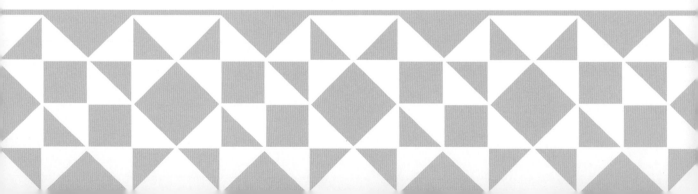

INTRODUCTION

Making a quilt is an absorbing and rewarding activity and, with a little bit of know-how, it is something anyone can achieve. With the help of this book, you will learn dozens of techniques so you succeed with your very first quilting project. Or, if you are a seasoned quilter, you may be inspired to learn or try a technique you never knew before.

By learning the skills needed for each project, you will feel comfortable with the different aspects of quilting. Becoming confident with your sewing machine and starting with some of the simple projects first will lead you through to completing more advanced patterns in no time at all.

In some cases, you will find several different options for completing parts of a project, such as attaching a binding. Try these out and see what suits your style and comfort level best. There is no right or wrong answer in quilting so just remember to adjust your fabric requirements if needed. If something doesn't look right, simply take it apart and try again.

Some people find choosing their fabrics to be a challenging part of the process, but with an understanding of the colour wheel you will soon be on your way to designing your own visually appealing quilts. A good starting point is to pick one fabric you like and build the design from there.

Quilting should be fun and relaxing, and if something doesn't work straight away, simply take a break and try again. Soon you will see how rewarding completing your first quilt is, and you will want to carry on making more beautiful projects to give as gifts or to keep for yourself and pass down through your family.

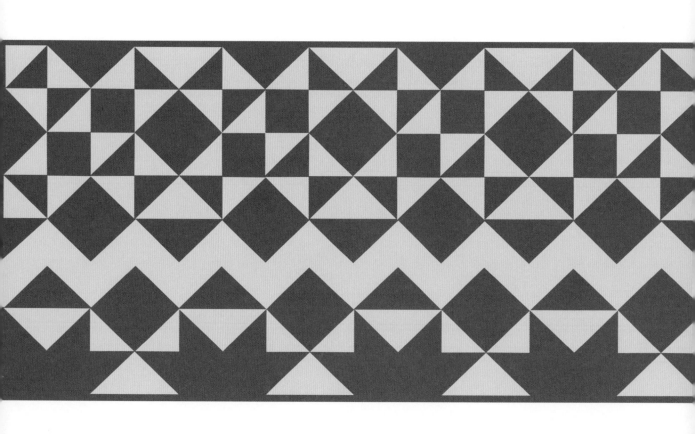

GETTING STARTED

TOOLS AND MATERIALS

Making a quilt does not require a lot of equipment. If you are a beginner, you probably won't need more than needles and threads or a sewing machine, scissors, pins, a ruler or measuring tape, a pencil, and a thimble. There is, however, an enormous selection of specialized tools that have been designed to make quilting easier.

▶▶ GENERAL SEWING EQUIPMENT

For quiltmaking you will need a set of hand-sewing needles – both "sharps" and "betweens". Both types come in several lengths, thicknesses, and eye size. Needles are sized by number: the higher the number, the finer the needle. Pins are essential for pinning the layers of a quilt together while you work. Always press seams as you go, with an iron or by fingerpressing.

Sharps
"Sharps" are standard hand-sewing needles and are usually used for processes such as tacking, hand piecing, and finishing the edge of binding.

Betweens or quilting needles
Shorter than sharps, these allow quick, even stitching for hand quilting and appliqué.

Quilter's pins
Long quilter's pins are useful for holding the layers of a quilt together as you work. Flower-headed pins are easy to pick up.

Glass quilter's pins
Glass-headed pins are easy to handle and are not affected by a hot iron. These are extra long for quilting, too.

Glass-headed straight pins
Ordinary dressmaking pins are used to hold pieces together during hand piecing.

Safety pins
If the layers of the quilt are not too thick, you can use ordinary safety pins to hold them together.

Hera
A plastic, blade-like device for creasing a temporary line on the fabric. A small wooden "iron" or chisel can also be used.

Iron
It is essential to press seams as you work, so have an iron and ironing board set up in your work area.

Curved safety pins
These are most commonly used for pin-tacking the layers of a quilt. The curve helps prevent the layers from shifting.

Thimble
Made from metal, leather or suede, plastic, or a combination, a thimble protects the middle finger when pushing the needle through the fabric.

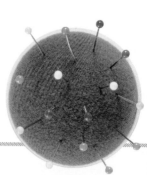

Pin cushion
Pin cushions range from traditional emery-powder-filled shapes to magnetic pin-catchers. Magnetic types can interfere with the smooth operation of computerized sewing machines.

➤▶SEWING MACHINE

You can use any modern sewing machine for quilting as long as you can adjust the stitch length and the machine has a zigzag function. Other useful features to look for are feed dogs – the toothed bars in the needle plate that feed the fabric through – that can be dropped, and a large throat area – the area between the needle plate and the machine's horizontal arm. This is useful when working on a bulky item. Needle sizes are in metric (e.g. 70) and universal/American (e.g. 10). For quilting you will need a range of needles in sizes from 70/10 to 90/14, depending on your project.

FEET
All sewing machines come with a standard presser foot as well as a selection of specialized feet for different purposes. You should have a 6mm (¼in) seam foot for piecing patchwork. Also useful for quiltmaking are:

Walking foot
This strange-looking foot "walks" across the fabric, so that the upper layer of fabric is not pushed forward. When used for quilting, it also guides the layers of fabric and wadding through the feed dogs at an even speed. Also commonly known as an even feed foot.

Zip foot
This foot fits to either the right- or left-hand side of the needle and is normally used for stitching close to the teeth of a zip. If you are finishing the edges of a quilt with piping, it enables you to stitch close to the piping cord.

Darning foot
Also known as a free-motion quilting foot, this foot "floats" on a spring mechanism for free-motion quilting of fancy patterns. The clear acrylic foot gives you a good view of your stitching area.

▶▶ MEASURING TOOLS

Many of the basic measuring tools that a quiltmaker
needs are standard items in a home office or workshop.
Others can be found in a general sewing kit.

Tape measure
An essential item
for quiltmaking and
patchwork. Many
have metric as well
as imperial markings.

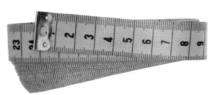

T-square
Useful for squaring corners
and measuring.

Set square
Useful for measuring and
ensuring square corners on
quilt blocks, and for cutting
individual pattern pieces.

Seam gauge
With its centimetre
and inch markings,
this is very useful
for measuring and
marking small
measurements
such as seam
allowances.

Quilter's ruler
Useful for drafting patterns and templates, as well
as for determining seam allowances. Quilter's
rulers can be square, rectangular, or triangular.

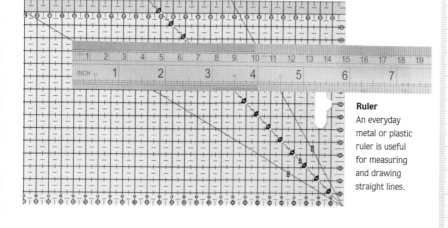

Ruler
An everyday
metal or plastic
ruler is useful
for measuring
and drawing
straight lines.

▶▶ MARKING TOOLS

Various pencils and pens are used to draw designs and mark seam allowances on both paper and fabric. Some, such as tailor's chalk and removable markers, are non-permanent.

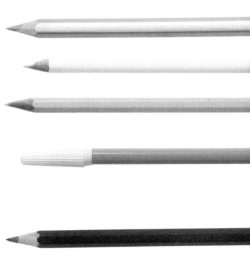

Soft pencils
Have a selection of these. Light-coloured pencils show up well on darker fabrics or paper when tracing or transferring patterns or designs.

Water-soluble pen
Marks made by a water-soluble pen are removed with a dab of water or by washing.

Hard pencil
Use a hard pencil with a fine point for drawing around templates.

Low-tack masking tape
Ideal as a guide for straight lines on large pieces of fabric, it should be removed promptly after use.

Tailor's chalk
This is available in a range of colours and the marks it makes are easily brushed away.

▶▶ TEMPLATES AND STENCILS

The most durable templates and stencils are cut from translucent template plastic, rather than card. Cut using a sharp scalpel to ensure accuracy. Freezer paper can also be used to create templates and is especially useful in some appliqué work.

Ready-made window template
Made from sturdy template plastic or metal, a window template is used to mark both the outline and the seamline without the need for two templates.

Freezer paper
The shiny side sticks to fabric when ironed and can be reapplied several times. It is handy for appliqué.

Ready-made quilting stencil
A quilting stencil can be used to transfer a pattern onto the fabric. Trace the stencil design with a water-soluble pen.

Card
Stiff card can be used to make templates but will not last as long as plastic.

Tracing paper
This is essential for tracing motifs or pattern pieces onto template plastic or card before cutting out.

Other useful items for quiltmaking include graph paper, dressmaker's carbon paper, slivers of soap, flexible curves, drawing compasses, protractors, and erasers, which can all help with designing and transferring pattern pieces or motifs.

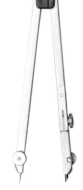

Flexible curve
This is a useful device for marking curved shapes such as semi-circles.

Geometry compass
Very useful for drafting templates with curves and for drawing circles and semi-circles.

Isometric paper
This paper is for drafting triangles, hexagons, and diamonds. It is very useful for English paper piecing.

Graph paper
Useful for planning blocks and quilt layouts, and for rescaling designs.

Eraser
A useful item to have to hand when drawing or tracing designs.

Dressmaker's carbon paper
This is a permanent method of transferring designs to the wrong side of the fabric, using a marking wheel or pencil.

⊠▶CUTTING EQUIPMENT

Scissors are absolutely essential in quiltmaking and you should have at least three pairs: one dedicated to cutting fabric; one for paper or card and wadding; and a small, sharp pair for snipping threads. A rotary cutter speeds up fabric cutting.

Small sharp scissors
Use for snipping thread ends, clipping seams, and trimming seam allowances. A specialized version of small scissors called appliqué scissors can be helpful in appliqué work. The blades are curved to protect fabric that is not being trimmed from being damaged by sharp points, but appliqué scissors should not be seen as a replacement for ordinary small scissors.

Pinking shears
Useful for cutting fabric that tends to fray.

Cutting shears
These come with blades of varying lengths. Buy good-quality shears, ideally ones that can be resharpened.

Seam ripper
Used for removing stitching that has gone awry. It incorporates a small cutting blade.

Rotary cutter
Used with a quilter's ruler and self-healing mat, this makes light work of cutting fabric, and especially of cutting through many layers at the same time. Handle with caution.

Craft knife
This is invaluable for cutting stencils from template plastic. Never use it on fabric.

Self-healing mat
Marked with a grid in 2.5cm (1in) increments, the surface "heals" itself after cutting with a rotary cutter, leaving it smooth and without any notches or grooves that might catch the cutter next time you cut. Do not use with a craft knife.

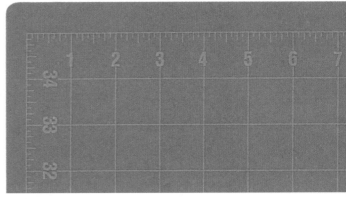

▶ THREADS

There are so many threads available and knowing which ones to choose can be confusing. There are specialist threads designed for special tasks, such as machine embroidery or quilting. Threads also vary in fibre content, from pure cotton to rayon to polyester. Some threads are very fine while others are thick and coarse. Failure to choose the correct thread can spoil your project and lead to problems with the stitch quality of the sewing machine. For piecing, it is important to match the thread to the fabric, such as cotton with cotton, to ensure they both shrink at the same rate. Match the colour to the lighter fabric or use a neutral shade. For appliqué, match the thread colour to the piece being stitched. Speciality threads include silk, metallics, and rayon.

COTTON THREAD
A 100 per cent cotton thread. Smooth and firm, this is designed to be used with cotton fabrics and is much favoured by quilters.

SEWING THREAD
Threads come in a dazzling choice of colours, types, and weights. Sewing thread is used for hand- and machine-sewing.

QUILTING THREAD
Quilting thread is heavier than sewing thread and is waxed to prevent breaks.

POLYESTER ALL-PURPOSE THREAD
A good-quality polyester thread that has a very slight "give", making it suitable to sew all types of fabrics. It is the most popular type of thread.

SILK THREAD
A sewing thread made from 100 per cent silk. Used for machining delicate fabrics. It is also used for tacking or temporary stitching in areas that are to be pressed, because it can be removed without leaving an imprint.

TOPSTITCHING THREAD
A thicker polyester thread used for decorative topstitching and buttonholes. Also for hand sewing buttons on thicker fabrics and some soft furnishings.

METALLIC THREAD

A rayon and metal thread for decorative machining and machine embroidery. This thread usually requires a specialist sewing-machine needle.

MACHINE EMBROIDERY THREAD

Often made from a rayon yarn for shine. This is a finer thread designed for machine embroidery. Available on much larger reels for economy.

HAND EMBROIDERY THREADS

Hand embroidery threads can be thick or thin. They can be made from cotton, silk, and linen as well as synthetic fibres. Some threads are single ply, while others are spun in multiple and can be divided into single strands: the fewer the filaments, the finer the embroidery line.

Pearl cotton
This is a strong, glossy thread with a twisted construction. It comes in three weights: No. 3 (the thickest), No. 5 (which comes in the greatest range of colours), and No. 8 (the finest).

Stranded cotton floss
This versatile thread consists of six fine strands of lustrous, mercerized cotton, which can easily be separated if desired.

TYPES OF FABRICS

The fabrics you choose to use for your project can make a world of difference to the final outcome. A single pattern can look completely different across many quilts depending on the fabric patterns and types used and how they are put together.

Quilting cotton

The usual fabric of choice when making a quilt is a good-quality cotton. Quilting cotton has a higher thread count than many other cottons, which means it is both strong and wears well. Available in solid colours as well as numerous prints, there are thousands of options to choose from. It's a good idea to pre-wash quilting cotton and to buy more than your pattern requires as it can shrink by up to 5 per cent.

Denim

Denim is a versatile choice, especially for projects that will receive a lot of use. Because of its weight it causes bulky seams and it is not suitable for hand quilting. When sewing denim by machine, use a special denim needle with a walking foot. New denim should always be pre-washed to remove excess dye.

Organza

A sheer fabric that can be used to add an artistic touch when layered over other fabrics.

Wool

Available in a variety of weights and colours, wool is a warm, durable, natural fabric. Heavy-weight wool can be difficult to patchwork with but can make interesting appliqué. Any unfelted wools must be dry cleaned.

Velvet

The nap of velvet can make it difficult to work with and attention must be paid to the direction of the nap when cutting and joining pieces. Velvet usually requires dry cleaning. Iron carefully so as not to destroy the nap. Always sew in the direction of the nap and use a fine needle.

Linen

Made from the flax plant, linen is a cool, breathable fabric that is perfect for quilting. It is available in many different weights and can sometimes be found blended with cotton (cotton-blend). It can be expensive and difficult to work with. Always pre-wash and zigzag stitch the raw edges to minimize fraying.

Calico

Calico is traditionally a simple, inexpensive, plain or unbleached cotton fabric. In contemporary quilting terms, however, calico can also refer to the print on the fabric rather than the fabric itself; meaning an all-over, small print, usually of a floral pattern.

Muslin

This soft, loosely woven cotton fabric is generally white or natural in colour and comes in a variety of different weights. It is typically used as a foundation fabric when foundation piecing. Good-quality muslin also makes a lovely backing fabric.

Hand-dyed and batik

With one-of-a-kind patterns, hand-dyed fabrics are becoming very popular among quilters thanks to their uniqueness. A variety of different fabrics are available hand-dyed, but cotton is best for quilting. Variations in colour and pattern can occur across a cut of hand-dyed fabric. Always pre-wash hand-dyed fabrics using a dye magnet – a product that picks up the loose dye – and a colour fixer.

Corduroy

Corduroy is soft and durable, but due to the nap and the ribs, it can be difficult to work with. Narrow-rib and pinwale corduroy are the best choices for quilting. Always use a walking foot and pre-wash the fabric. Iron carefully so as not to destroy the nap.

Blends

Many fabrics are available as a blend between two different fibres. A fabric blend can often offer the best of both in one. For example, a silk-blend will be less expensive than a pure silk fabric.

❱❱ PRE-CUT AND RECYCLED FABRIC

Pre-cut fabrics are a package of coordinating fabrics from a manufacturer that have all been cut to the same size. This makes them very handy for patchwork projects in which you'd like a large variety of fabrics, but without buying fabric from the bolt. The popularity of pre-cut fabrics has grown dramatically in the last few years. Manufacturers have increased their ranges available in pre-cuts as well as the available shapes they produce. Many manufacturers have patterns made specifically from pre-cuts. Nowadays you can easily find Charm Squares™, Layer Cakes™, Jelly Rolls™, and even pre-cut triangles and hexagons in local shops and online. Using these pre-cuts is a quick and easy way to layout and sew together a quilt in hours, rather than days.

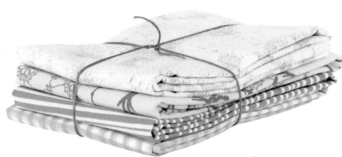

Fat quarters

Fat quarters are the most common type of pre-cut referring to a quarter-yard cut of fabric. A normal quarter-yard cut off the bolt would give you 23 x 112cm (9 x 44in), but a fat quarter is a 46cm (18in) cut from the bolt, which is folded selvedge to selvedge and trimmed in half down the middle to give you a 46 x 56cm (18 x 22in) piece of fabric, although sizes can vary slightly from manufacturer to manufacturer. Fat quarters are sometimes more useful than a 23cm (9in) cut from the bolt, as they allow for a larger pattern repeat.

Fat eighths

Fat eighths are half of a fat quarter (⅛ yard), measuring approximately 23 x 56cm (9 x 22in), rather than a typical ⅛ yard cut off the bolt, which would give you 12 x 112cm (4½ x 44in) of fabric.

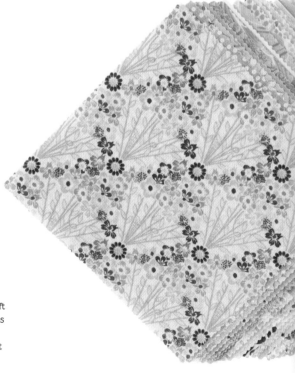

Recycled fabric

The very first quilts were often made from whatever worn-out fabrics were available, giving them a second life and saving money. Recycled fabric can be salvaged from almost anything. A slightly stained shirt, old table linen, or denim from jeans can be used to create a personal project. Very often the fabric is well-broken-in giving it a soft feel and heirloom appearance. It also usually will not shrink any further or leach dye as it has most likely been laundered on many previous occasions. Take care when adding recycled fabrics to any project, as the weight of the fabrics may be different from that of the other fabrics you are using.

Diecut

Diecuts are specific shapes cut by the manufacturer. Hearts and hexagons are popular shapes, but they can be almost any other shape and come in a variety of sizes. Diecuts are often useful for appliqué projects.

Jelly Roll™

Jelly Rolls™ are pre-cut collections of 6.5 x 112cm (2½in x 44in) fabric strips. The strips are cut selvedge to selvedge across a piece of fabric. A Jelly Roll™ typically contains 40 strips of fabric, but this can vary from manufacturer to manufacturer.

Layer Cakes™

Layer Cakes™ are pre-cut 25.5cm (10in) squares from a designer's range of fabric. They contain one print of each pattern and colourway in the line. Depending on the range, they typically have 36–42 squares in a pack.

Charm Packs™ and Mini Charm Packs™

Charm Packs™ and Mini Charm Packs™ are the same as Layer Cakes™, but smaller in size. Charm Packs™ measure 12.5cm (5in) squares and Mini Charm Packs™ measure 6.5cm (2½in) square.

WADDINGS AND FILLINGS

Wadding is the soft middle layer between the quilt top and the backing that gives a quilt its plushness and warmth. It is available in a variety of different materials and thicknesses, depending on your preferences and needs. Knowing a little about what options are available will help you choose the right wadding or filling for your project. Always follow the manufacturer's instructions for washing and quilting the wadding you choose.

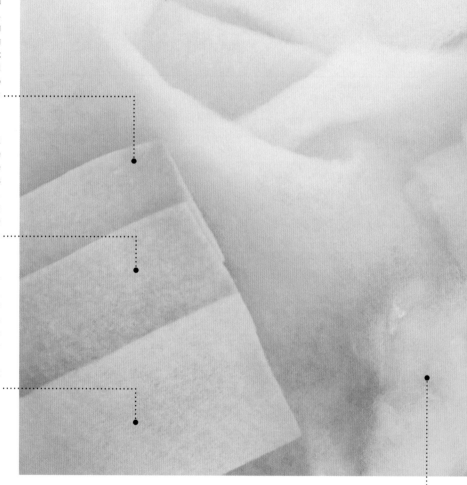

Cotton
100 per cent cotton is a natural, warm, and breathable choice. Cotton wadding can shrink significantly during washing (about 5 per cent), which gives the quilt a slight texture and a more traditional look. Because of this you may wish to pre-wash it.

Poly/cotton blend
A synthetic/natural blend gives you the best of both worlds. These waddings are machine washable and will not shrink as much as 100 per cent cotton waddings. The cotton part may shrink during washing though, so it may be wise to pre-wash it.

Polyester
Polyester waddings are light in weight, available in many thicknesses, and usually inexpensive. But being synthetic, they do not breathe well and are more flammable than a natural wadding; therefore, they are not recommended for baby quilts. They do not shrink, so you should not need to pre-wash.

Toy filling
The most commonly used and inexpensive type of toy filling is made from polyester, but cotton (including organic cotton), wool, and even bamboo are also available.

Bamboo

Natural and eco-friendly, bamboo is soft and strong. It generally has a low loft and will not shrink very much. Bamboo blends are also available, often as a 50/50 cotton blend.

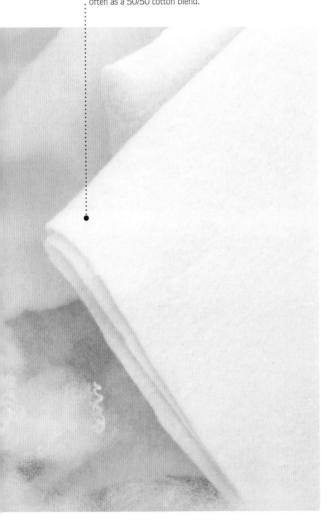

LOFT

Loft, or weight, refers to the thickness of a wadding. The higher the loft, the thicker the wadding, and the warmer the quilt. A low-loft wadding is typically less than 6mm (¼in) thick and is easy to quilt. A medium-loft wadding is about 6–12mm (¼–½in) in thickness and can still be machine or hand quilted. A high-loft wadding is generally over 1.2cm (½in) and is difficult to quilt. It should therefore be held together with evenly spaced ties (see p.137).

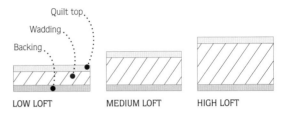

Quilt top
Wadding
Backing

LOW LOFT   MEDIUM LOFT   HIGH LOFT

QUILTING YOUR WADDING

The product label on your wadding should state the amount of space you can have un-quilted between quilting stitches for that specific type of wadding. If you are planning to have limited quilting on your quilt, you should take this into consideration when choosing your wadding to make sure it can accommodate the design. The distance can vary significantly, anywhere from approximately 5–25cm (2–10in), depending on what the wadding is made of and how it has been formed.

BUYING WADDING

Wadding is available to buy off the bolt in different widths and often in pre-cut standard bed quilt sizes. When buying wadding, you need to know the finished size of the quilt you are making first. The wadding should be at least 15cm (6in) larger in both width and length than the finished quilt top, to allow it to overhang on all sides when making your quilt sandwich (see p.44).

If you're not able to find a piece of wadding that is wide enough to fit your quilt, you will need to buy enough wadding so that you can piece together several lengths to meet your requirements. You can piece the wadding with either a vertical or horizontal seam depending on which will result in the least waste.

A QUILT EXPLAINED

The terms patchwork and quilting are very often confused with one another. Patchwork usually refers to piecing, or sewing, pieces of fabric put together to make a larger, more intricate, piece of fabric. The quilting is the stitches that hold the three layers of a quilt together. Read below to find out more about how a quilt comes together and its different elements.

▶▶ THE FIVE ELEMENTS OF A QUILT

There are five main elements needed to complete a quilt. The first element is a finished quilt top, often made of patchwork or appliqué. Your quilt top can be assembled using a repeating block pattern or several different blocks, such as in the diagram. You can also add sashing and borders (see pp.78–83) to either make the quilt fit a specific dimension or enhance the design.

The second element is wadding. Most quilters prefer to use 100 per cent cotton wadding or a 50/50 blend of cotton and silk, or cotton and bamboo. See pages 22–23 for more information on waddings.

The third element is the backing, which needs to be larger than both the quilt top and the wadding. A quilt back can be made of a single print or pattern, or it can be pieced just like the top. Very often several pieces of fabric will need to be joined to make a large enough backing for a quilt (see p.45).

The fourth element is quilting. Quilting is a very important part of a quilt and has a double duty. The main purpose is to hold all three layers of the quilt (the "quilt sandwich") together securely. The second purpose is to create texture. The more a project is quilted, the more stiff it will become. A loose stitched pattern will give the quilt more softness. Quilting can either be done by hand or machine (see pp.130–133, 134–137).

The fifth and final part of a quilt is the binding. The binding is a strip of fabric sewn around the perimeter of the quilt to enclose the raw edges (see pp.46–51). A traditional binding should be finished at the back by hand. This method will give the quilt a professional finish.

QUILT SANDWICH

The term "quilt sandwich" refers to the three basic layers in a quilt: the backing, wadding, and quilt top. Starting with the backing and quilt top as the bottom and top layers, the wadding is then placed between them to complete the sandwich. Once all of the layers have been stitched together, or quilted, the sandwich is squared up and the raw edges are enclosed with a binding.

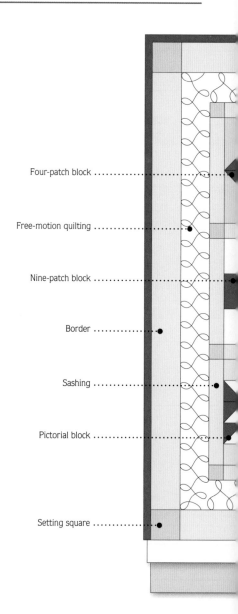

Four-patch block ....

Free-motion quilting ....

Nine-patch block ....

Border ....

Sashing ....

Pictorial block ....

Setting square ....

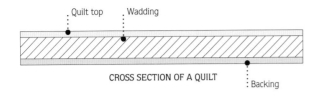

Quilt top   Wadding

CROSS SECTION OF A QUILT

Backing

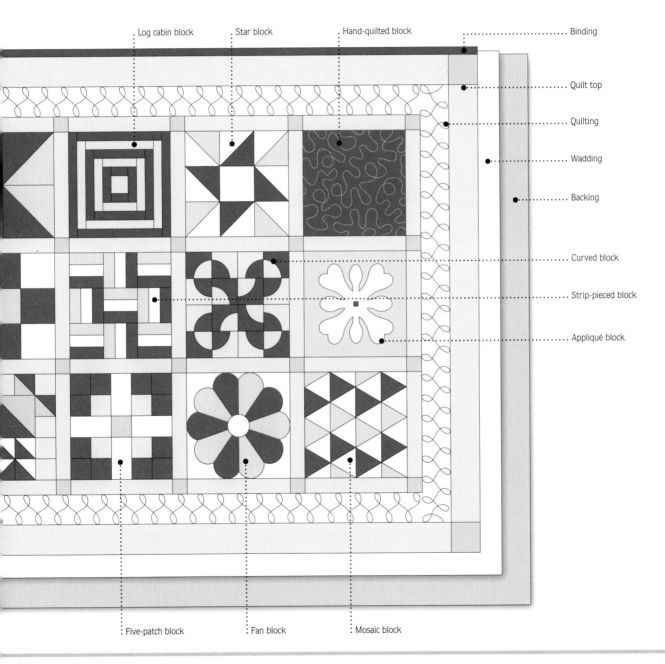

Log cabin block

Star block

Hand-quilted block

Binding

Quilt top

Quilting

Wadding

Backing

Curved block

Strip-pieced block

Appliqué block

Five-patch block

Fan block

Mosaic block

QUILT SIZES AND MEASUREMENTS

Standard bed sizes vary around the world, so depending on where you live you may need to adapt a pattern to fit your specific needs. Mattress depth is another factor that can vary significantly and will influence the way your finished quilt looks on a bed. A deep mattress will make a quilt look much smaller than a shallow mattress of the same size. Follow the simple instructions below to measure up your bed for the perfect quilt size.

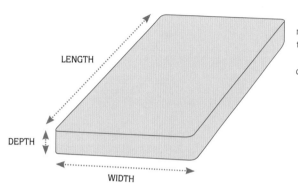

To calculate the quilt size needed for a specific bed, you will need to accurately measure the bed itself. Do so by using a measuring tape to record the width, length, and depth of the mattress. Using these three measurements you can design and fit a quilt to any size mattress.

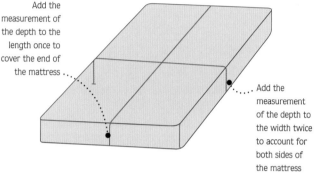

Add the measurement of the depth to the length once to cover the end of the mattress

Add the measurement of the depth to the width twice to account for both sides of the mattress

When calculating the depth of the mattress be sure to add the measurement of the depth twice to the width (one for each side of the quilt) and only once to the length (for the bottom).

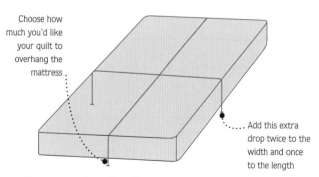

Choose how much you'd like your quilt to overhang the mattress

Add this extra drop twice to the width and once to the length

If you want the quilt to hang or drop below the mattress, you will need to add a few additional centimetres (inches), depending on your requirements. You will need to add the drop twice to the width and once to the length, as above.

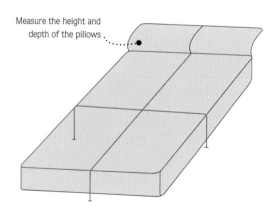

Measure the height and depth of the pillows

To add a pillow tuck to your quilt you will need to add approximately 45cm (18in) to the length of your quilt. Measure the height and depth of the pillows to be covered, then add a few extra centimetres (inches) to allow for the tuck.

⧩▶ ADAPTING A PATTERN

Once you have determined the dimensions of the quilt you'd like to make, you may need to make some adjustments to the pattern. If you are making a quilt without a pattern you may also find the following information helpful.

NUMBER OF BLOCKS

Most quilts are made from blocks of one size. Once you have determined the size of the finished block (the size minus seam allowances), divide the total width of the quilt by that block size to find out how many blocks you will need per row. Then, divide the total length of the quilt by the block size to determine how many rows you will need. Chances are these numbers will not come out evenly, so round both numbers down. Multiply the two numbers together to determine the total number of blocks you will need for your quilt top.

MAKING UP THE DIFFERENCE

If the measurements for the number of blocks needed did not come out evenly there are several ways to remedy this. Adding borders around the quilt top (see pp.80–83) to make up the difference is the easiest way. Adding sashings between the blocks, or making them wider if they are already part of the design, can also make up the difference (see pp.78–79), but this will alter the look of the quilt top. The third, and most difficult, option is to change the size of the blocks until they meet your requirements.

FABRIC REQUIREMENTS

If altering a pattern, it is important to take these changes into consideration when purchasing your fabrics for the quilt. It is usually a good idea to purchase more fabric than you need anyway, to allow for shrinkage during pre-washing and also for any mistakes when cutting or sewing. Don't forget to add any extra fabric you might need for the backing and binding, too.

Determine how you'd like the quilt to sit on the bed, as well as what it will be used for. For example, baby quilts are very often too small for a standard size bed, but still add a personal touch when on display.

Most quilts hang a bit below the depth of the mattress. The type of bed should also be taken into consideration when planning your quilt. Daybeds will only need extra to hang down on one side, for example.

DESIGN PRINCIPLES

Most patchwork and many appliqué quilts are based on patterns comprised of blocks – that is, squares made following the same pattern, which are then assembled to make the quilt top. This means that they can be broken down into working units that are easier to cope with than a large overall design. There are hundreds of existing block designs that you can make in fabrics and colours of your own choice (see pp.54–57) but, once you understand the basic principles, it's fun to design patterns of your own.

▶▶ USING TEMPLATES

Some elements require templates, which are copies of the pieces of the pattern. Ready-made templates are available. Find out if the seam allowances have been added. Elements to be machine pieced must include the exact seam allowances, while appliqué patterns and those for hand piecing do not need a precise allowance, but are generally cut larger than the finished shape. Many templates are cut with a "window" that shows the area of fabric you will finish up with; this also enables you to mark the seamline and the cutting line without moving the template. Alternatively, you can make your own templates following these instructions.

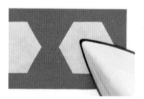

Limited-use templates using freezer paper: Trace the pattern pieces onto freezer paper and cut them out. Iron the waxy side onto the wrong side of the fabric and then cut out around the shape.

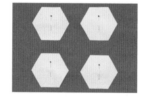

Limited-use templates using tracing paper: Pin the template in place and cut out the shape, again adding the seam allowances by eye.

Durable templates using heavy card: Draw the shapes on paper or tracing paper. Cut them out, draw around them again on heavy card, and cut them out, or glue the shapes to the card and cut out.

Durable templates using template plastic: Trace the shapes directly onto the template plastic, or cut the desired shapes from paper and glue them to template plastic. Cut them out with paper scissors.

PLANNING YOUR OWN BLOCKS

The main patchwork block categories are four-patch (see p.54), nine-patch (see p.54), five-patch and seven-patch (see p.55). Each one lends itself to certain finished block sizes. Four-patch patterns can always be divided by even numbers, while nine-patch blocks are easiest to work with if the finished size is divisible by three. Five-patch and seven-patch patterns are more limited; they are multiples of 5 x 5 and 7 x 7 units (or patches) per block respectively.

If you want to design your own block pattern, start by deciding what size you want your finished block to be and draw it on paper, sub-dividing it into the relevant number of patches. Further sub-divide each patch into strips, triangles, smaller squares, or rectangles to create your design. When you are satisfied, transfer each element to another piece of paper and add a seam allowance to each side of each separate element.

With appliqué patterns, enlarge or reduce the pattern if necessary (see p.34) and copy it onto tracing paper. Decide which elements should be cut as separate pieces and trace them individually onto another piece of tracing paper so they can be cut out and used as patterns.

Many blocks can be super-sized by dramatically increasing the dimensions of a single block, making quilts of an ideal size for baby quilts. Combining several of these bigger blocks allows the quick creation of a full-size quilt.

➤▶ UNDERSTANDING COLOUR

Understanding the basic principles of colour theory is crucial to designing a successful quilt. Even a simple design gains impact from good colour choices. The three primary colours (red, yellow, and blue) can be placed side by side to create a colour wheel. When two primary colours are combined, they create "secondaries". Red and yellow make orange, yellow and blue make green, and blue and red make purple. Intermediate colours called tertiaries occur when a secondary is mixed with the nearest primary.

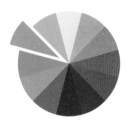

Monochromatic designs: These use different versions of the same colour. So a quilt based on greens will not stray into the other sections of the colour wheel, but will only use green fabric.

Complementary colours: Colours that lie opposite one another on the wheel, such as yellow and violet, or red and green, are called complementaries. They provide contrasts that accent design elements and make both colours stand out. Don't forget black and white, the ultimate opposites.

Analogous colours (side by side): Starting with a primary or dominant colour, expand in each direction on the colour wheel by one colour. Similar to a Monochromatic colour scheme, but with a bit more variation.

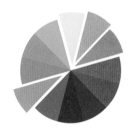

Analogous with complementary: Similar to an Analogous colour scheme, but with the addition of a complementary primary colour. The addition of a complementary colour provides a nice contrast to the analogous colour grouping.

Triadic: A triadic or triangle uses three colours that are evenly spaced out around the colour wheel. This offers a strong contrast while retaining a harmony among the colours. On the colour wheel above, every fourth colour is grouped.

COOL

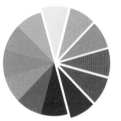
WARM

Temperature: The temperature of a colour can usually be described as cool or warm. You can split the colour wheel in half between the green, blue, and blue-violet – cool – side and the yellow, red, and red-violet – warm – side. Cool colours will tend to recede and do well in the background while warm colours will advance and give the feeling of closeness.

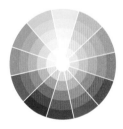

Tint, shade, and tone: When you add white to a colour it is called a tint of the colour and when you add black to a colour it is called a shade of a colour. Adding both black and white to a colour is called a tone of the colour and will leave the colour with a grey quality.

SCALE, PRINTS, AND DESIGN

There are so many quilt designs and fabrics to choose from that getting started on designing your quilt can be a bewildering experience. Most quilts are a mixture of printed and plain fabrics. When using prints, first consider whether the pattern lends itself to being a primary or secondary pattern. The plain areas will act as a foil. Using a design wall can help with your planning.

THE SCALE

The size of the image – its scale – is an important factor when working with print fabrics. A large-scale pattern is generally more difficult to work with, but it can be used successfully, especially in bigger blocks.

Try combining large prints, especially conversation prints – prints that have themed motifs – with plain fabrics. Large prints are useful for making quick-and-easy baby and children's quilts. Medium-scale prints can be fussy cut (see p.38) quite effectively, and small-scale patterns are usually simple to use as they can be cut into small units that have a consistent look.

There are also hand-dyed and batik fabrics (or fabrics printed to look as if they are hand-dyed) and tone-on-tone fabrics that have tiny motifs printed on a background of the same colour that look almost like plain colours from a distance. These give more visual texture than a solid plain colour and can really help to bring a design to life.

GEOMETRIC-PATTERNED FABRICS

Fabrics such as stripes, checks, and tartans can make fascinating secondary patterns when they are cut and re-assembled. Widely used in country-style quilts, they need careful handling in order to be most effective. Stripes, in particular, can be set in different directions to create visual movement within a block, while checks and tartan can be combined with each other or with plain fabrics to great effect. Be careful to align stripes and checks when cutting and sewing.

BORDERS AND SASHING

A plain colour can act as a foil to a busy print, giving the eye somewhere to rest and providing the keen quilter with a place to show off skills. Plain sashing (see p.78) can direct a viewer to the block pattern within, and while borders can be patterned and pieced, plain borders frame and contain a quilt in a special way. Balance – between prints and plains, lights and darks, warmth and coolness – is key to any successful design, and the more quilts you look at, and make, the better your judgement will become. One way to work is to choose a main print first and then coordinate the plains and other prints around it.

CREATING A DESIGN WALL

Using a design wall is a good way to test how fabrics will look as it allows you to step back and view different options from a distance. Hang a plain white sheet over a door to make a temporary design wall, or fashion a moveable one from foam board covered with white flannel over a layer of wadding. If you have room for a permanent design wall, mount cork or foam board on a wall in your sewing area and pin fabrics to it.

Stripes
Stripes add interest that varies depending on the way the fabric is cut. Striped fabrics can be cut with the stripe, across the stripe, or at an angle to the stripe.

Plains
Plain fabrics are often used as the basis of a quilt design, as borders, and for the quilt backing.

Check fabric
Checks work well combined with plains for simple patchwork or quilting designs.

Small-scale prints
Many small-scale prints almost give the effect of plain fabrics, but with extra interest. You may have to take care aligning the pattern where two pieces with the same pattern meet.

Large-scale prints
Large-scale prints work best in large blocks. Individual motifs can be cut out and used in appliqué, or can be fussy cut for patchwork.

Medium-scale prints
Ideal for patchwork, medium-scale prints can be successfully combined with plain fabric and small-scale prints for texture and interest.

GENERAL TECHNIQUES

Quiltmaking involves different techniques at different stages, but many techniques are the same, whether the quilt is pieced, appliquéd, or wholecloth. The techniques outlined in this section are key, whichever type of quilt you choose to make. You will use them over and over again.

▓▶ PRE-WASHING AND PREPARING FABRICS

While many people are divided on whether to pre-wash fabric or not, if you plan to wash a finished project in the future it is usually a good idea to pre-wash the fabrics before you cut or sew them together. Different fabrics shrink at different rates, so pre-washing will help avoid uneven shrinkage, and therefore puckering, when the finished item is first washed. Pre-washing fabrics can also help to remove any excess dye, which can leech out and discolour the other fabrics. Small pre-cuts do not need to be washed before use as the washing process may ruin them. Check before pre-washing any pre-cut fabrics.

PRE-WASHING FABRICS

There are many things to consider when deciding whether to pre-wash your fabrics or not:

Shrinkage The quality and type of fabric will yield different percentages of shrinkage. You can expect the shrinkage of cotton to be anywhere from 3mm (⅛in) to 1.2cm (½in). If you choose not to pre-wash your fabric, but do wash them in the future, the fabrics may pucker or distort as they each shrink at different rates and in different directions to one another. Therefore, a quilt made from pre-washed fabrics will stay flatter and look more even after washing. However, many people prefer this crinkly look and feel it gives a quilt a vintage feel. Most manufacturers' washing instructions are given on the bolt, so note these down when purchasing the fabric.

Bleeding While it is not a guarantee, pre-washing a fabric may help to remove any excess dye from it. Certain colours – such as reds, blues, and purples – are more prone to bleeding than others. You can test a small piece of the fabric for colourfastness by submerging it in a clear bowl of warm, soapy water and leaving it to sit. After about 30 minutes to an hour, place the bowl on a white surface and check to see if the water has changed colour. If the water has, you know that the item is not colourfast and will bleed when washed. If the water has not changed colour, leave the wet piece of fabric to sit on a scrap of white fabric. If the colour transfers to the white fabric after a short period of time then the fabric is not colourfast. If it does not, the fabric is colourfast.

If the fabric is not colourfast, you should pre-wash it several times using a dye magnet or colour catcher. After each wash cycle, perform the colourfastness tests to check if any dye still remains. Continue to pre-wash the fabric until it no longer bleeds. You can also buy colour fastener to treat a fabric. Follow the manufacturer's instructions.

Handling and chemicals Fabric right off the bolt usually contains sizing and other chemicals to help protect it. These make the fabric easier to cut and machine sew, but may not be suitable for people sensitive to chemicals. If you pre-wash it to remove the chemical, pressing your washed fabric well will help to set the fibres and allow for more precise cutting and piecing.

What will the finished item be used for? If you are making an item for display, such as a wall hanging, there may be no need to pre-wash the fabrics, as they will probably never be washed in the future.

NEW FABRIC

WASHED FABRIC

This swatch shows what can happen to a piece of cotton fabric during washing. Some of the dye bled out and the fabric shrunk.

TIPS FOR PRE-WASHING

• **You should pre-wash fabric** in the same manner you intend to launder the finished item in the future. For example, if you plan to wash the finished quilt on a cold wash cycle and dry it on a medium dryer setting, you should pre-wash the fabric in the same way.

• **You can serge or zigzag stitch** along the cut edges of some looser weave fabrics before washing to help prevent them from unravelling during pre-washing.

• **Always pre-wash large pieces** of fabric when you first buy them, so you don't forget to do it when you work with them at a later stage.

• **When pre-washing fabric**, snip off a small triangle at each corner to prevent fraying. Washing small pieces of fabric in a lingerie bag will help prevent fraying.

• **Hand-dyed or Batik fabric** should always be washed and dried to set the dyes and keep them from running and fading. Use a dye catcher to help prevent the excess dye from spoiling the colours around them.

PREPARING FABRICS

After it has been washed, there is not much that needs to be done to fabric before you use it, but there are a few things to keep in mind:

Drying If using a tumble dryer, dry your pre-washed fabrics on a medium heat setting and remove them from the dryer before they are completely dry. Drying a fabric completely can set the wrinkles firmly into the fabric and make them difficult to remove.

Ironing Iron the fabric straight out of the dryer while it is still damp. Starching the fabric can make the ironing easier and more effective.

Cutting Before you cut, check the straight of grain is true by checking it against the selvedge of the fabric.

TIPS FOR PREPARING

• **Cut quilt borders on the lengthways grain** to minimize stretching.

• **To find the lengthways grain**, pull the fabric gently along both straight grains. The stretch will be greater along the weft, or widthways, grain.

• **Try to position any bias edges** away from the edges of a block to minimize stretching and to keep the size of the block accurate.

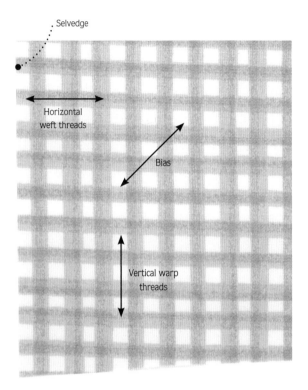

Selvedge

Horizontal weft threads

Bias

Vertical warp threads

Each fabric has three grains: the lengthways grain (warp), which runs parallel to the selvedges; the horizontal grain (weft), which runs perpendicular to the selvedges; and the diagonal grain (bias). The rigid edge on each side is called the selvedge. The bias should be handled carefully as it stretches easily, which can lead to distortions in the patchwork.

◢▶ ALTERING THE SIZE OF A MOTIF

The easiest way to alter the size of a motif is to use a photocopier. Whether enlarging or reducing, divide your desired size by the actual size of the template.

Multiply that figure by 100 to give the percentage of the enlargement or reduction you will need. You can also use gridded paper to alter the size of a motif, as below.

1 For non-geometric motifs, trace the outline onto gridded paper. To make a pattern twice the size of the original, draw a grid double the size on another piece of paper. If you start with 1.2cm (½in) squares, for example, increase the size of each square in your new grid to 2.5cm (1in).

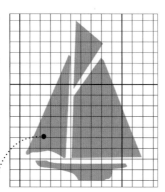

The original motif traced onto paper gridded into 1.2cm (½in) squares.

2 Transfer the lines within each square of the grid so they correspond to the lines of the original motif. When you have finished, trace the motif onto a new piece of paper to smooth out any distortions. You are now ready to transfer the newly sized motif to a template.

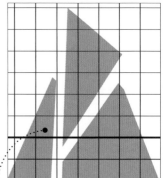

The motif enlarged onto a 2.5cm (1in) grid.

◢▶ ROTARY CUTTING

Many of the most popular patterns can be rotary cut. You will need a rotary cutter, a quilter's ruler, and a self-healing mat. When cutting a square into other shapes, such as half-square triangles that will be

reassembled into a square, you must start with a square that is larger than your finished square will be, to allow for the seam allowances. Always keep your fingers away from the cutting edge.

CUTTING A STRIP

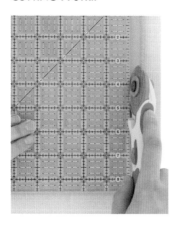

1 First you must straighten the edge of the fabric. Fold the washed and pressed fabric so the selvedges are together. Place it on the mat, with the folded edge aligned with the top of the ruler. Lay the ruler on top and cut along the edge of the ruler, away from your body, to remove the selvedges. Keep the hand holding the ruler steady.

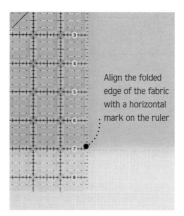

Align the folded edge of the fabric with a horizontal mark on the ruler

2 Turn the mat so as not to disturb the newly cut edge and reposition the ruler over the area of fabric that is to be your strip. Align the ruler carefully along the cut edge to give the desired width and line up the folded edge with a horizontal mark on the quilter's ruler. Cut the fabric strip along the grain.

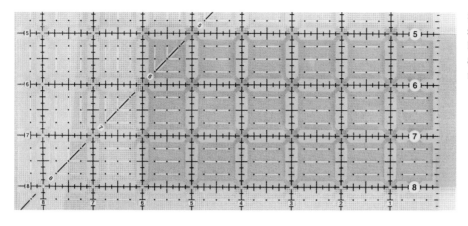

3 To cut the strip into smaller units, position it horizontally on the mat and measure using the ruler grid. Cut as before.

CUTTING SQUARES AND RECTANGLES

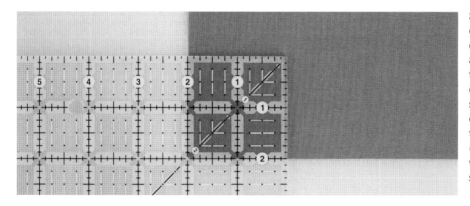

Squares and rectangles can also be cut using a quilter's ruler, which has a guideline marked across the diagonal from corner to corner. Add a 2.2cm (⅞in) seam allowance when cutting a right-angled triangle and a 2.75cm (1⅜in) seam allowance when cutting a quarter-square triangle.

CUTTING A PIECED STRIP INTO SMALLER STRIPS

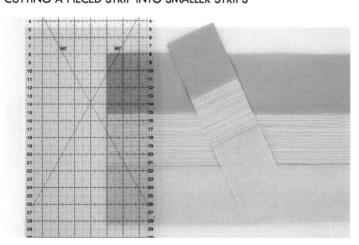

Press your pieced strip and position it right side up horizontally on the mat. If necessary, straighten the pieced strip at one end, as in Step 1 of Cutting a strip (see opposite). Turn the strip and reposition the ruler over the area that you want to use. Cut pieced strips of the desired width.

CUTTING A PIECED STRIP ON THE BIAS

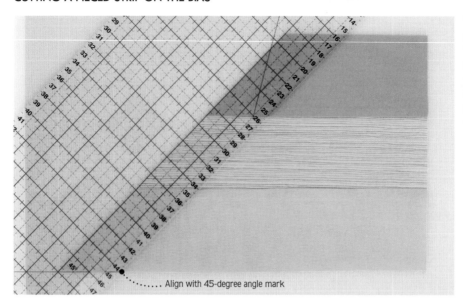

.... Align with 45-degree angle mark

Trim one end of the pieced strip at a 45-degree angle, using the line marked on the quilter's ruler. Cut strips of the desired width at the same angle by measuring along the straight edge of the ruler.

CUTTING TRUE BIAS STRIPS

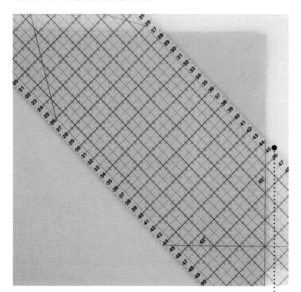

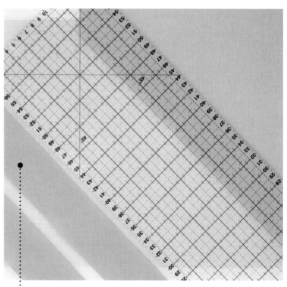

1 Straighten the edge of the fabric as in Step 1 of Cutting a strip (see p.34). Align the 45-degree mark on the ruler with the straightened edge and cut away the top corner of the fabric along the ruler.

2 Align the ruler with the cut edge and cut strips of the desired width, as in Cutting a pieced strip on the bias, above. Be careful when using bias strips as the 45-degree cut brings stretch to the fabric.

CUTTING HALF-SQUARE TRIANGLES

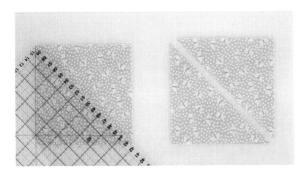

Cut half-square triangles across the diagonal of a square. Remember to cut the square large enough so that it includes a seam allowance.

CUTTING QUARTER-SQUARE TRIANGLES

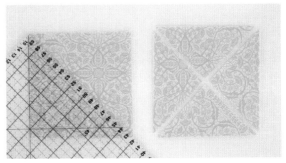

Cut a square diagonally from both corners to create four quarter-square triangles. Again, include a seam allowance when cutting the square.

CUTTING IRREGULAR TRIANGLES

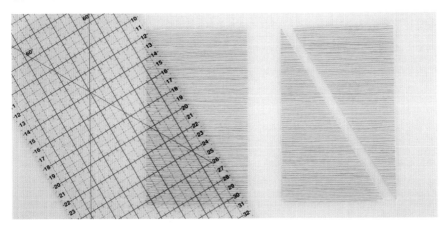

Cut a rectangle across the diagonal to create two irregular long triangles. To make a matching pair of irregular triangles, cut another rectangle across the diagonal, starting at the opposite corner.

CUTTING 45-DEGREE DIAMONDS/TRIANGLES

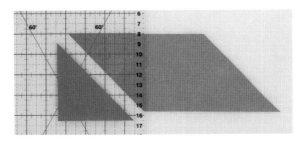

Cut a strip the desired width of the diamond, plus the seam allowances. Cut a 45-degree angle at one end. For the second cut, align the quilter's ruler along the cut edge according to the width of diamond required.

CUTTING CURVES

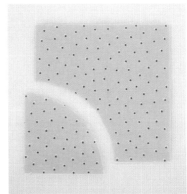

Gentle curves can be cut with a rotary cutter, but it is advisable to use a small blade. Blades are available in standard 25, 45, and 90mm (1, 1¾, and 3½in) sizes.

▶ CUTTING BY HAND

Quiltmakers generally cut with scissors if the pieces are small or intricate, or if they have unusual angles or shapes. Appliqué motifs are almost always best cut by hand. You should keep at least one pair of good-quality, sharp dressmaker's scissors just for cutting cloth. Do not cut paper, template plastic, wadding, and the like with your fabric scissors. Most quiltmakers have several pairs of scissors in different sizes.

CUTTING WITHOUT A PATTERN

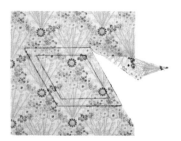

1 Mark the outline of the shape to be cut on the wrong side of the fabric and add the seam allowance, if you wish.

2 Cut out the shape along the marked cutting line – or cut a short distance away, if you have only marked the stitching line.

CUTTING WITH A PATTERN

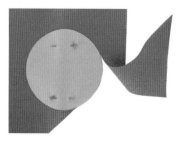

Patterns made from paper are familiar to dressmakers and can provide an easy way for quiltmakers to cut the same shape several times over. Pin the pattern to the fabric and cut around it, adding the seam allowance if necessary.

FUSSY CUTTING

This is a method of isolating particular motifs in printed fabric and cutting them so they show as a feature in a block of patchwork or appliqué. It can seem wasteful of fabric, but the results are usually worth it. It is easier to delineate the area you want if you cut a window template to the desired size and shape.

▶ UNPICKING A SEAM

Everyone makes the occasional mistake and sometimes seams must be unpicked; moreover, some patterns depend on taking out seams during construction. It is vital that the unpicking process does not stretch the edges of the fabric. Unpicking works best on seams that haven't been pressed. Never use scissors to unpick a seam.

METHOD 1

1 Working from the right side, insert the point of the seam ripper into the stitches to cut the thread.

2 Pull the layers of fabric apart gently as you work to the end of the seam.

METHOD 2

1 Working from the wrong side, hold the seam taut and insert the seam ripper into every third or fourth stitch to cut the thread. Work your way along the seam.

2 Hold the lower piece of fabric flat and pull gently on the top piece to separate the two. Do not use this method on bias seams.

➤ STARTING AND FINISHING

Securing the thread at the beginning and end of any stitching is, of course, essential. Traditional hand sewing begins and ends with a knot at the end of the thread, but knots can interfere with quilting and sometimes show on the top of the quilt. There are several knots that are useful for quiltmaking. Backstitched loops (see p.40) lie almost flat and are a secure way of finishing off a seam.

THREADING A NEEDLE

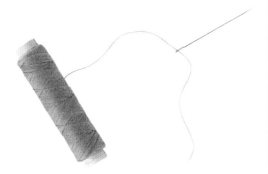

1 Trim the end of the thread. Insert the end of the thread through the eye of the needle, then cut to the desired length from the spool. Because of the way thread is twisted as it is made, threading the needle with the end that comes off the spool first will help prevent tangles.

2 After threading, run the thread between your thumb and forefinger in the direction that the thread came off the spool to smooth it.

TIPS

• **Thread weight:** Use a thread weight that is appropriate to the size of the needle and a needle size that is suited to the weight of the fabric.
• **Thread length:** Keep the thread length to no more than 50cm (20in) long; it will be less likely to kink and fray.
• **Needle threader:** Use a needle threader if you have difficulty getting the thread through the eye.
• **Cutting direction:** Always cut away from your body when possible.
• **Knot size:** Knots make lumps wherever they occur, so make sure that knots are as small as possible so that they can be hidden easily.

WRAPPED KNOT

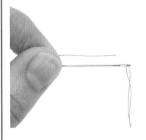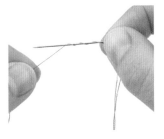

1 Thread the needle, then hold one free end of the thread parallel with the needle, as shown.

2 Take hold of the free end of the thread securely and wrap it around the needle a few times.

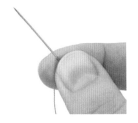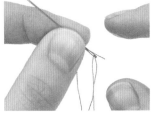

3 Slide the wraps towards the eye of the needle and hold them with your thumb and forefinger.

4 Grab the wraps between your index finger and thumb of the opposite hand.

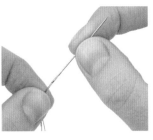

5 Slide the wraps down the end of the needle, over the eye and down the thread.

6 Keep pulling the knot down the thread until it reaches near the bottom of the length of thread.

BACKSTITCHED LOOP

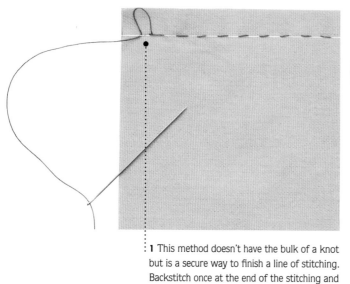

1 This method doesn't have the bulk of a knot but is a secure way to finish a line of stitching. Backstitch once at the end of the stitching and pull the needle through; do not pull the thread taut, but leave a small loop of thread.

2 Take the needle through the loop, then pull the thread tight.

DOUBLE BACKSTITCHED LOOP

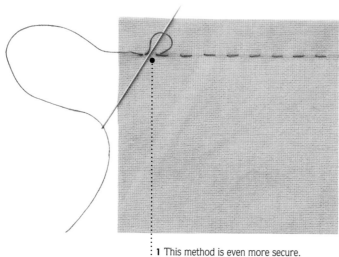

1 This method is even more secure. Backstitch once at the end of the line of stitching, leaving a small loop of thread as in Step 1 of Backstitched loop (see above). Insert the tip of the needle through the loop and pull it through to form a second loop, creating a figure of eight.

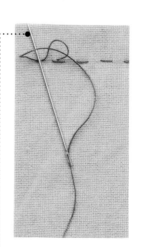

2 Insert the tip of the needle through the second loop.

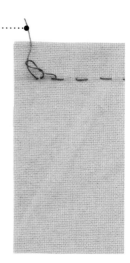

3 Pull the thread taut to form a knot.

❯❯ HAND STITCHES FOR QUILTMAKING

Although most quilts today are made on a machine, there are a number of techniques that require hand sewing; it is important to choose the correct stitch for the best result.

RUNNING STITCH

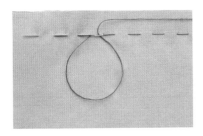

This is the most common stitch for hand piecing. Take the needle in and out of the fabric several times, making small, evenly spaced stitches. Pull the needle through gently until the thread is taut, but not tense. Repeat to the end of the seam.

STAB STITCH

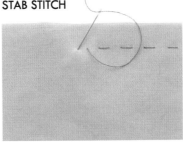

This popular quilter's stitch is useful for sewing through several layers or into thick fabric. Take the needle vertically through the fabric layers from the top and pull until the thread is taut but not tense. For the next stitch, bring the needle through vertically from below. Continue sewing to the end of the seam.

BACKSTITCH

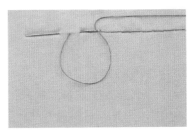

Backstitch can be worked in a row as an alternative to running stitch to join units together. Bring the needle through all the layers to the right side, then insert it a short distance behind the point where it emerged. Bring it back up to the right side again, the same distance in front of the point where it first emerged. Repeat to the end of the seam.

OVERSEWING

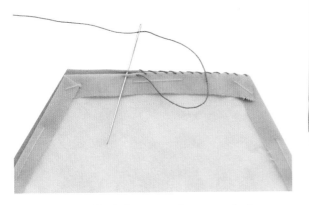

Also known as whipstitch or overcasting, oversewing is used to join two edges with an almost invisible seam. Bring the needle through the back edge to the front edge, picking up a few threads from each edge as you go. Pull gently on the thread until it is taut but not tense, and repeat.

SLIP STITCH

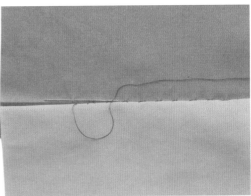

Used mainly in appliqué, slip stitch joins two pieces of fabric with an invisible line of stitching. Knot the thread and bring the needle to the front, hiding the knot in the folded edge of the top piece. Now pick up a thread or two on the back piece, then take the needle into the top piece right next to this stitch and slide it a short distance inside the fold. Bring the needle to the front again, then repeat, catching a few threads on the back piece with each stitch.

ᛥ▸ PRESSING

Pressing is essential when making accurate patchwork. It is different to ironing, which can cause fabric and seams to distort. When pressing, press down in one place, then lift the iron and move it before pressing down on another area. Set pieces aside to cool after each pressing and always press the seam towards the darker fabric to prevent darker colours from showing through lighter fabrics. The temperature of the iron should be appropriate to the fabric.

PRESSING STRAIGHT SEAMS

1 Place the unit or sewn strips with right sides together on the ironing board with the darker fabric on top. Press the iron along the seam, lifting the iron at regular intervals. This is called "setting the seam". It helps ensure accuracy by locking the threads in place and smoothing the fibres of the fabric.

2 Open the unit to the right side and press from one end to the other along the seam. If you keep the lighter piece nearest you and press with the tip of the iron, you can press the seam to the darker side at the same time as you open the unit.

PRESSING BIAS SEAMS

Work along the straight grain to prevent the seam from being pulled out of shape. Lift the iron and replace it rather than dragging it along the seam.

WORKING IN ROWS

Press the seams in adjoining rows in opposite directions from one another to minimize bulkiness where the seams join.

PRESSING A PIECED BLOCK

Place the block wrong side up on the ironing board. Do not press hard, but make sure the seams lie as flat as possible.

PRESSING SEAMS OPEN

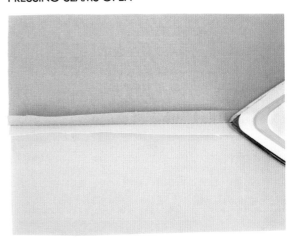

Where several seams meet, you may need to press seams open to reduce bulk. After setting the seam as in Step 1 of Pressing straight seams (opposite), turn the piece to the wrong side, open the seam, and press along the length with the tip of the iron.

THUMBNAIL

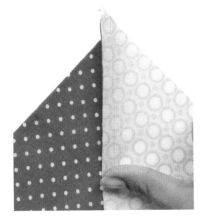

Work on a hard surface. Open the unit out and press first on the wrong side, then on the right side, running your thumbnail gently but firmly along the seamline and pressing the lighter fabric towards the darker fabric.

SMALL WOODEN IRON

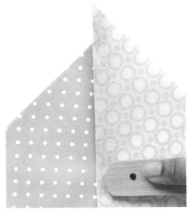

Working on the wrong side, place the flat, chisel-shaped edge of the tool on the seamline and run it gently along the seam.

HERA

A hera is a plastic, blade-like device. It is used in certain embroidery techniques but is also useful for creasing a temporary line on the fabric.

⧉▶ ASSEMBLING THE QUILT LAYERS

Once you have marked the quilting pattern on the quilt top, it is time to assemble the quilt "sandwich", which is the layers of top, wadding, and backing that make up the quilt. If the wadding has been folded, open it out flat and leave it for several hours to relax the wrinkles.

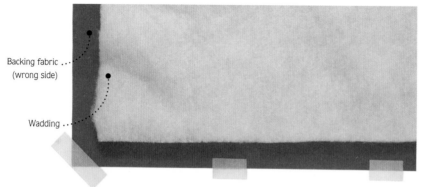

Backing fabric
(wrong side)

Wadding

1 Trim the wadding and backing 7.5–15cm (3–6in) larger all around than the finished top. Lay the backing wrong side up on the work surface and smooth it flat. Secure it to the surface with masking tape.

2 Centre the wadding on the backing, and smooth it out.

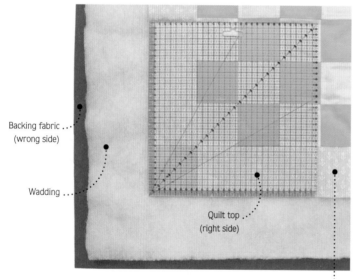

Backing fabric
(wrong side)

Wadding

Quilt top
(right side)

3 Position the quilt top right side up, centring it on the wadding. Use a ruler to check that the top is squared up. Using large quilter's straight pins, temporarily pin along each squared edge as you work.

4 Working from the centre out diagonally, horizontally, and vertically, tack or pin the layers together. Remove the pins along the edge as you reach them. Keep smoothing the layers. Take tacking stitches 5cm (2in) long – first vertically and horizontally, then diagonally. If pinning using safety pins, follow the same pattern and insert the pins at 7.5–10cm (3–4in) intervals.

▶▶ MAKING A BIGGER BACKING

Most bed quilts are wider than most fabrics, so it is often necessary to piece the backing. There are several ways to do this, but you should avoid having a seam down the vertical centre of the quilt.

1 Cut two full widths of fabric of the required length. Set one aside, and cut the other in half lengthways. Trim off all selvedges.

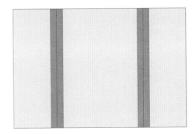

2 Add one half-width to each vertical side of the full width to get the required width.

▶▶ BAGGING OUT

Sometimes you may want to finish the edges of the quilt before you quilt it. The technique works well on smaller projects, such as baby quilts. Cut the wadding and backing slightly larger than the quilt top.

1 Centre the quilt top right-side up on the wadding. Centre the backing on the quilt top, right side down. Pin or tack the layers together around the edge.

2 Start machine stitching at the bottom edge, several centimetres (about an inch) from the corner, taking a 6mm (¼in) seam. Secure with backstitching.

3 At the corners, stop 6mm (¼in) from the edge with the needle down. Raise the presser foot. Pivot the fabric, lower the presser foot and continue sewing. On the fourth side leave an opening of 12–25cm (5–10in). Secure with backstitching.

4 Clip the corners to reduce bulk. If necessary, trim and grade the seams, then turn right side out through the opening.

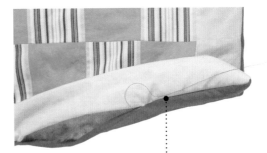

5 Level the edges on the inside. Pin or press lightly. Blind stitch the opening closed.

BINDINGS

Pre-made bias binding is available in various colours and widths, or you can make your own. Bindings should be applied as a continuous strip. If possible, cut straight binding strips along the lengthways grain of the fabric or join pieces before applying. Bias binding has more stretch than straight binding, making it suitable for binding work with curved edges.

MAKING A STRAIGHT BINDING STRIP

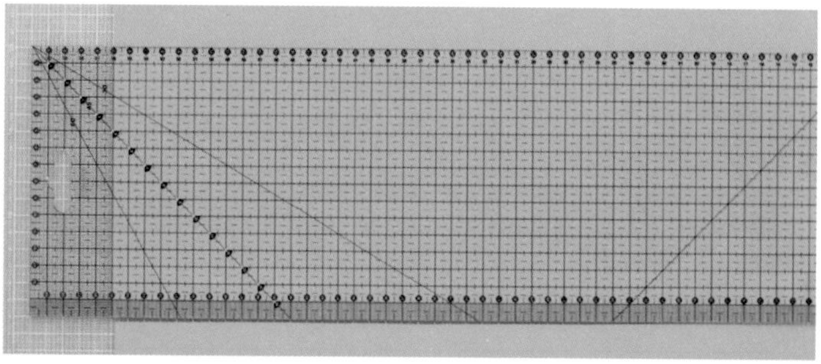

1 Measure the edges of the piece being bound and decide on the width of the finished binding. Cut strips six times this width plus an additional 1.2cm (½in), allowing extra length for mitring corners and joining pieces.

2 Ensure your edges are square and cut along the straight grain of the fabric. Add about 40cm (16in) extra to the length for full quilts, 30cm (12in) for baby quilts, wall hangings, and large embroideries, and 20cm (8in) for small works.

MAKING A BIAS STRIP

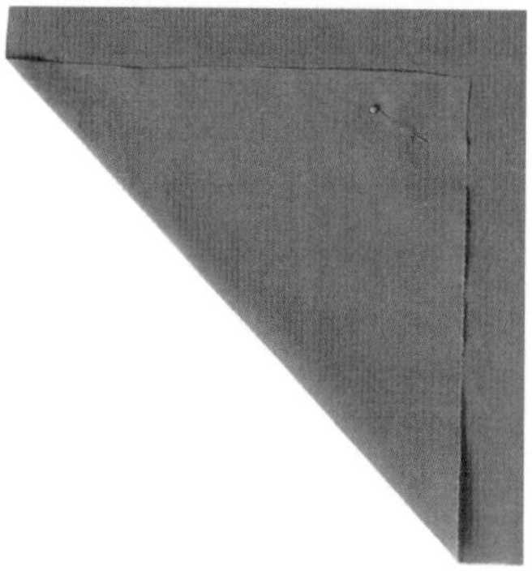

1 Buy at least 1.5m (59in) of fabric so you can cut very long strips. Cut off selvedges and smooth the fabric flat. Straighten the right-hand edge of the fabric, then fold this edge back so that it aligns with the top edge and forms an exact 45-degree angle. Cut along this bias fold.

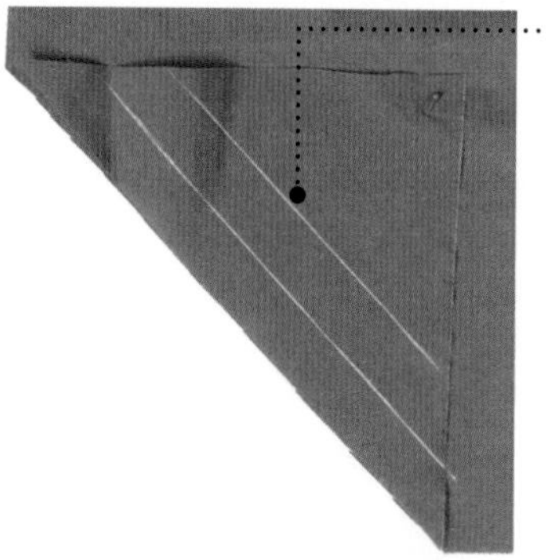

2 Using a metal ruler and a sharp piece of tailor's chalk, mark lines on the fabric parallel to the bias edge and 4cm (1½in) apart. Cut out the strips along the chalked lines. Cut as many strips as you need for your project plus a few extra.

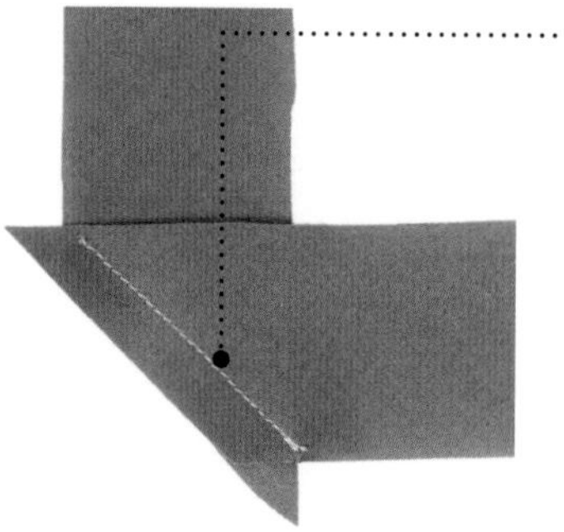

3 Join strips together to make a continuous strip. Pin the strips together at a 90-degree angle with right sides facing and sew a 6mm (¼in) seam on the bias. The seam should run from edge to edge of each strip, with a triangle of fabric left at either end of the seam.

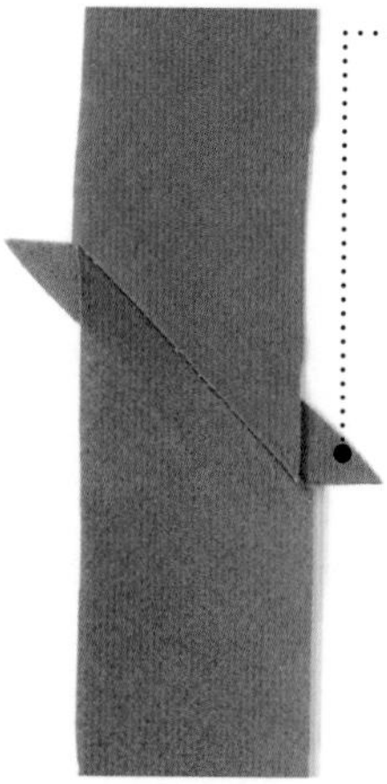

4 Press the seam open and trim off the seam allowances and the extending little triangles (dog ears). You can also make bias binding with these prepared strips. To do this, press under the edges or run the strip through a bias binding maker.

MAKING A CONTINUOUS BIAS STRIP

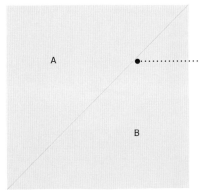

1 Cut a large square of binding fabric with 90-degree corners. Mark two opposite sides as A and B and draw a diagonal line. Cut along the marked line.

2 Place the two triangles right sides together as shown and join them along the overlapping edges using a tight stitch length. Press the seam open. Trim off the dog ears.

3 Mark lines parallel to the bias edges the desired width of the strip.

Mark parallel lines of desired width

4 Bring the remaining two straight-grain edges together and offset the marked lines by aligning one tip of the fabric to the first marked line on the other side. Pin carefully to match the marked lines and sew together, right sides facing, to make a tube.

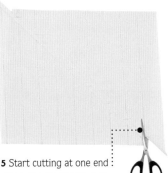

5 Start cutting at one end along the marked lines to make a continuous strip.

CALCULATING METERAGE
To calculate how much binding you can make from a piece of fabric, multiply the length of the fabric by the width of the fabric, then divide by the width of the cut binding strip.

For example, for a 5cm (2in) wide binding strip cut from a 90cm (36in) square of fabric you will get: 90 x 90cm = 8,100cm (36 x 36in = 1,296in). Divide by 5cm (2in) to get 1,620cm (648in). You can make 16.2m (18yd) of binding, which should be sufficient for a king-size quilt.

Always work in either the metric or the imperial system when doing your calculations.

◥▶BINDING WITH PRE-MADE BIAS BINDING

Every quilt will need some form of binding to finish the raw edges and a pre-made bias binding, or bias tape, is a quick and easy way to do this. Bias tape can be used on small projects and projects that will not receive a lot of wear, such as wall hangings. Steps 3–8 show how to mitre a corner when binding. Mitring should be used when attaching any binding around a corner.

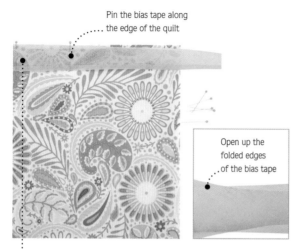

Pin the bias tape along the edge of the quilt

Open up the folded edges of the bias tape

1 After squaring up the quilt, measure all four sides, add them together, then add approximately 40cm (16in) to the total length. Cut the bias tape to this final measurement. Open up the long, folded edges of the bias tape and with right sides together, align the bias tape along one side of the quilt top, starting in the middle of the side, not a corner. Pin in place.

2 Beginning a few centimetres (inches) from the end of the bias tape, with the quilt right side up, stitch along the outside edge of the tape through all the layers. Use a seam allowance that is one-quarter the width of the open bias tape. The stitch should land approximately on the open fold of the binding.

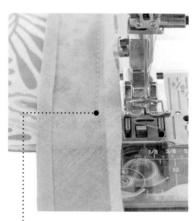

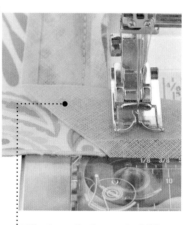

3 Carefully stitch along the edge stopping a seam allowance's distance from the corner. Back stitch a few stitches.

4 Remove the quilt from under the machine foot, but do not cut the threads or pull it out too far.

5 Create a mitred corner by folding the tape 45-degrees to the right of the quilt top. The tape should run parallel with the bottom edge of the quilt.

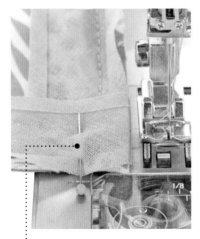  

6 Carefully fold the binding back 180-degrees to the left, aligning the edge with the bottom edge of the quilt. Pin as needed.

7 Turn the quilt 90-degrees and place it back under the machine, inserting the needle back into the same place you last finished sewing. Continue stitching down the second side.

8 Repeat the process for the remaining sides until you are approximately 30cm (12in) from your starting point. Measure the distance between the finishing point and the beginning end of the binding tape. Trim and connect the two ends of the tape so they fit along the final section, then finish stitching the binding in place along the edge.

Mitre the corner neatly ......

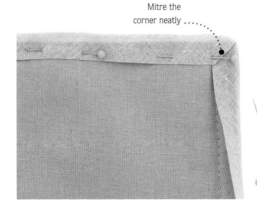 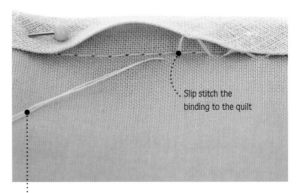

Slip stitch the binding to the quilt

9 Fold the binding to the back of the quilt, taking care to neatly mitre each corner as you do. Fold under the long raw edge of the binding tape that had previously been open. Pin the binding in place.

10 With a needle and thread, slip stitch the binding (see p.41) to the back of the quilt, enclosing the raw edges of the quilt sandwich and covering the stitches made from sewing the binding to the front. Secure tightly and finish by embedding the knot inside the quilt.

◥▶ TURNED-EDGE BINDING

Adding a turned-edge binding is a simple way of finishing off the edge of a quilt. The binding is formed by folding the backing of the quilt to the front. It has the appearance of traditional bias binding.

1 Pin the backing fabric out of the way and trim the wadding and quilt top so they are even and square with one another. Unpin the backing fabric and trim it to twice the width you want the finished turned-edge binding to be.

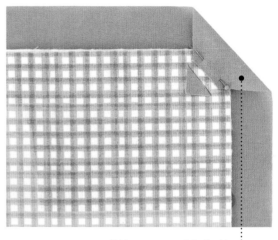

2 Fold one corner of the backing fabric over the corner of the quilt and pin it in place. Trim off the tip, as shown here.

3 Fold the adjacent edge of the backing fabric over so that it aligns with the cut edges of the wadding and the quilt top.

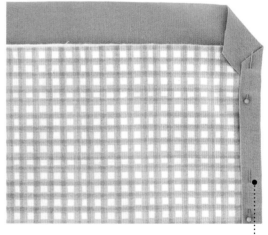

4 Fold the edge of the backing fabric over a second time so all the raw edges are enclosed. Neatly and evenly pin the folded edge in place along the entire length.

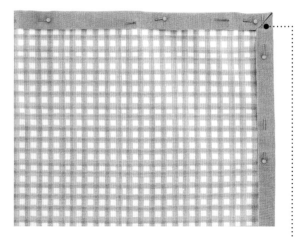

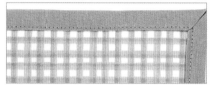

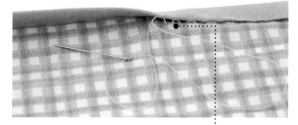

5 Repeat Steps 2–4 for the other corners and other edges, making sure adjacent edges meet in clean mitres at the corners, as shown here. If any trimmed corners from Step 2 are visible, you may need to trim them back some more.

6 Neatly slip stitch (see p.41) the turned-edge binding to the quilt top or, for a much quicker finish, you can machine topstitch along the edge of the binding (see inset).

DOUBLE-FOLD BINDING

Double-fold binding is stronger than bias tape binding (see pp.48–49) and is recommended for binding bed quilts. Quilted wall hangings and other small, layered items that won't get routine wear and tear can be bound with a pre-made bias tape.

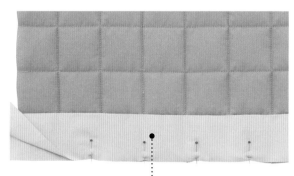

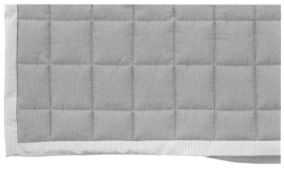

1 Cut strips of binding fabric six times the desired width of your finished binding, plus 6mm (¼in) extra. Cut enough strips to fit around the perimeter of the quilt top, plus approximately 40cm (16in) extra. Join them all together (see p.46). Fold the strip in half lengthways, wrong sides together, and press.

2 Lay the doubled binding strip on the right side of the quilt, raw edges to raw edges. Pin the binding strip in place along the first side, starting about halfway down the side, and checking that none of the joined binding seams land on a corner. If they do, reposition the binding and pin again.

3 Start machine stitching about 20cm (8in) from the start of the binding using the seam allowance of the desired width of the binding. Stitch along the raw edges, mitring the binding when you reach a corner, then pin and continue to sew the next side (see pp.48–49) until all sides have the binding attached. Join the ends in your preferred method.

4 Turn the folded edge of the binding to the back of the quilt, taking care to mitre the corners on the back too. Neatly slip stitch (see p.41) the binding in place.

PATCHWORK

PATCHWORK BLOCK GALLERY

There are hundreds of traditional patchwork patterns and we have space to show only a few – but once you've mastered the basic construction techniques, you will be able to look at a block pattern and work out both the constituent elements and how to piece it together.

▶ FOUR-PATCH BLOCKS

The simplest four-patch blocks are made up of just four squares (patches), but those four squares can also be created by piecing together two half-square triangles, or four quarter-square triangles, or various combinations thereof.

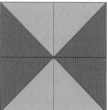

YANKEE PUZZLE

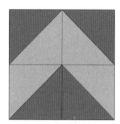

CHEVRON OR STREAK OF LIGHTNING

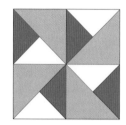

BROKEN PINWHEEL

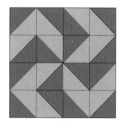

FLYFOOT

▶ NINE-PATCH BLOCKS

Nine-patch blocks are made of nine units in three rows of three. By adding a third colour to a simple nine-patch of two colours, you can create myriad variations.

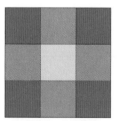

RED CROSS – THREE-COLOUR NINE-PATCH

THREE-COLOUR DOUBLE NINE-PATCH

ROCKY ROAD TO CALIFORNIA

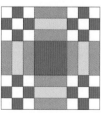

BUILDING BLOCKS

▶ PICTORIAL BLOCKS

Patchwork pictorial blocks tend to be highly stylized, with the individual elements of the design being made up of square and triangle units in varying combinations.

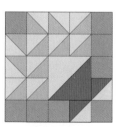

GRAPE BASKET

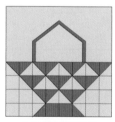

COLONIAL BASKET

BASKET OF SCRAPS

HOUSE WITH FENCE

▸▶ FIVE- AND SEVEN-PATCH BLOCKS

Five-patch blocks consist of a grid of five units in each direction, or 25 units in total, while seven-patch blocks have no fewer than 49 units (seven in each direction).

With so many elements, each one of which can be sub-divided in several ways, there is almost infinite scope for creating different patterns.

STAR AND CROSS PATCH

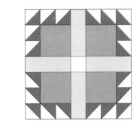

DUCK AND DUCKLINGS

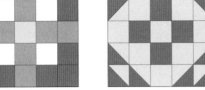

HENS AND CHICKENS

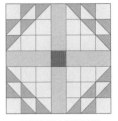

DOVE IN A WINDOW

▸▶ STRIP-PIECED BLOCKS

Strip-pieced patterns can be put together in random colour and fabric combinations or in repeating patterns. If two fabrics are pieced A–B–A and B–A–B, the resulting squares can be alternated to create a

basketweave block, similar to the one below. Seminole bands can be angled or set square and are wonderful for creating pieced border strips.

BASKETWEAVE

STRING-PIECED DIVIDED SQUARE

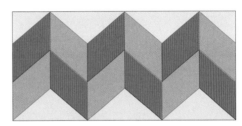

DOUBLE CHEVRON SEMINOLE

▸▶ LOG CABIN BLOCKS

There are many variations in log cabin blocks and settings. Strips of light and dark fabrics can be alternated, placed on adjacent or opposite sides, made of varying widths, or pieced from a combination

of smaller squares and rectangles. The centre square can be pieced, turned "on point", or made from a rectangle, triangle, or diamond.

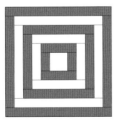

CABIN IN THE COTTON

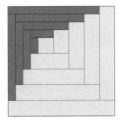

THICK AND THIN

CHIMNEYS AND CORNERSTONES

PINEAPPLE

⏵▶STAR BLOCKS

There are probably more kinds of star blocks than any other patchwork motif; the construction ranges from simple four-patch stars to extremely complex designs created by cutting 60-degree diamonds in half lengthways or crossways. The basic eight-point star alone, with its 45-degree angles, is the starting point for numerous variations, including the intricate lone star.

REPEATING STAR

EVENING STAR – MORNING STAR

CONSTELLATION BLOCK

BRACED STAR

CARD BASKET

EISENHOWER STAR

TENNESSEE STAR

SILVER AND GOLD

NINE-PATCH STAR

OZARK DIAMONDS

LONE STAR

TRAILING STAR

TIPS FOR MAKING BLOCKS

• **When marking,** make sure the marker has a sharp point. If you mark with dashes, not a continuous line, the fabric is less apt to shift or stretch.

• **Remember the rule:** measure twice, cut once. And bear in mind that measurements from one brand of ruler or mat are not always exactly the same as another brand. For accuracy, try to use the same ruler and mat, as well as the same machine foot, throughout the piecing process.

• **If you make** a sample block to begin, you can measure your finished blocks against it to ensure accuracy.

• **Whenever possible,** sew a bias edge to a straight edge to minimize stretching.

• **If you need** to trim a block to make it smaller, trim back an equal amount from all sides to keep the design of the block accurate and centred.

▶ CURVED BLOCKS

Probably the most popular of all traditional curved blocks is the drunkard's path (see pp.86–87). When the orientation or colour values of the four units is altered, a number of complex curving patterns result. Changing the size and shape of the curves alters the block considerably.

FALLING TIMBERS

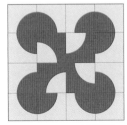

WONDER OF THE WORLD

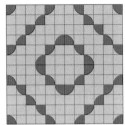

CHAIN LINKS

DRUNKARD'S PATH

ROBBING PETER TO PAY PAUL

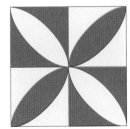

ORANGE PEEL

▶ MOSAIC BLOCKS

Though many of these can be machined, most are made by piecing together geometric shapes using the English paper-piecing method (see p.88). The most familiar block is grandmother's flower garden.

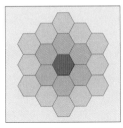

GRANDMOTHER'S FLOWER GARDEN

1,000 PYRAMIDS

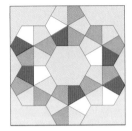

TUMBLING BLOCKS

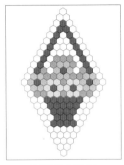

FLOWER BASKET

▶ FAN BLOCKS

Fans are based on quarter-circles and can be arranged in a number of different ways. However they are arranged, a curving pattern results. Variations such as Dresden plate patterns are full circles and are often appliquéd to a background. The segments can be curved or pointed, or both. The centre can be open to allow the background to show through or applied separately for contrast.

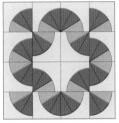

MOHAWK TRAIL

DRESDEN PLATE

PIECING

Piecing, or sewing pieces of fabric (units or patches) together, lies at the heart of patchwork. In fact, piecing is, simply, creating patchwork. First you join smaller pieces, then you join these to make your final design. You can choose between hand and machine piecing. Piecing by machine obviously produces faster results.

▶▶ HAND PIECING

Mark all seamlines on the wrong side of the fabric to give you an accurate guide to where to sew. Take care when sewing seams on bias-cut edges (for instance on diamond, triangle, or hexagon shapes) or around curves, as the raw edge is prone to stretching. Secure the seam with a small backstitch each time you bring the needle through and use a double backstitched loop (see p.40) at the end of a bias seam; do not sew into the seam allowance.

JOINING TWO UNITS WITH A STRAIGHT SEAM

1 Place the two units to be joined right sides together. You must not sew across the seam allowance of the adjacent seam, so mark that seam allowance with pins at the start and end points of the seam you are about to sew. Add more pins along the seamline you are about to sew, making sure that the seamline aligns on both units.

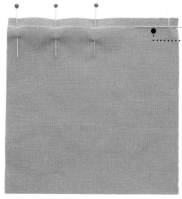

2 Remove the first pin and take the needle through both the front and the back units at that point. Secure the thread with a knot or take a couple of tiny backstitches into the seam allowance.

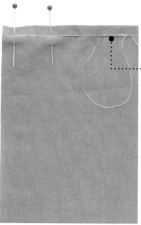

3 Take several short running stitches along the seamline, then pull the needle through. Repeat along the length of the seam, removing pins as you work.

4 From time to time, check the back of the fabric to make sure that your stitching is on the seamline on both sides. Stop at the end point marked with a pin in Step 1. Finish with a couple of backstitches to secure the thread.

JOINING HAND-PIECED ROWS

When joining rows of hand-pieced units together, you must avoid sewing into the seam allowances, just as you did when hand piecing two units together (see Joining two units with a straight seam, opposite).

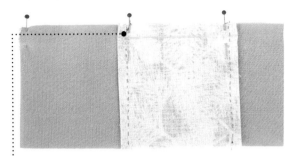

1 Place two rows of hand-pieced units with right sides together. Match the seamlines front and back, and pin through both layers at each corner at the start and end points (see Step 1, opposite). Align the seamlines and pin at intervals to hold the rows in place.

2 Start sewing at one end, working as for straight seams (see opposite), until you reach the first seam intersection. Sew through the start and end points but do not sew across the seam allowance.

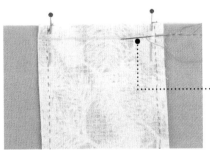

3 Make your first stitch in the second pair of units a backstitch right next to the seam allowance.

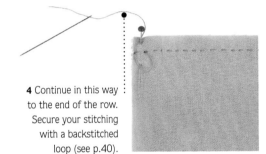

4 Continue in this way to the end of the row. Secure your stitching with a backstitched loop (see p.40).

5 Open the joined rows out and press the seams on each row to opposite sides. Press the just-completed seam to one side.

⏩ MACHINE PIECING

Stitching patchwork pieces by machine is a quick way of assembling a piece. As for hand piecing, always ensure that your fabrics are aligned with right sides facing and with raw edges matching. Leave a 6mm (¼in) seam allowance unless otherwise specified, and use a standard straight stitch.

JOINING TWO OR MORE STRIPS

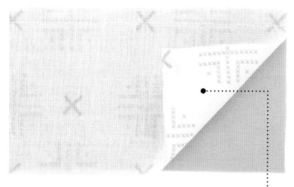

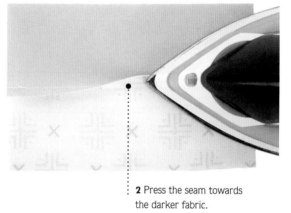

1 Place two strips of fabric right sides together, raw edges aligned. Sew a straight 6mm (¼in) seam along the length of the strip.

2 Press the seam towards the darker fabric.

3 When piecing several strips together, each time you add a strip, reverse the direction of your sewing; this helps to keep the strips straight and prevents the fabric from bowing. The seams should all be pressed in the same direction. The pieced strip can be cut into pieced units, which can then be combined to make a new pattern.

CHECKING SEAM ALLOWANCES

Rectangle A,
3.8 x 6.4cm
(1½ x 2½in)

Rectangle B,
3.8 x 6.4cm
(1½ x 2½in)

Rectangle C,
3.8 x 6.4cm
(1½ x 2½in)

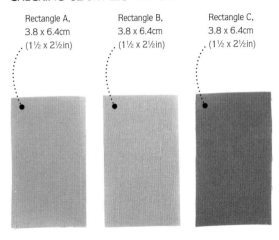

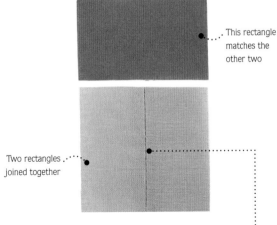

This rectangle matches the other two

Two rectangles joined together

1 When sewing any pattern, for your finished pieces to fit together well, it is important to ensure you sew using the correct seam allowance. One way to check that your machine is sewing a standard 6mm (¼in) seam allowance is to cut three pieces of fabric, A, B, and C, each 3.8 x 6.4cm (1½ x 2½in).

2 Pin and sew rectangles A and B, right sides together, along their long edges. Press the seam to one side. If your seam allowance is accurate, rectangle C should be an exact size match to the joined pieces, as shown. If it is not, adjust the needle position until the seam allowance is accurate.

CHAIN PIECING

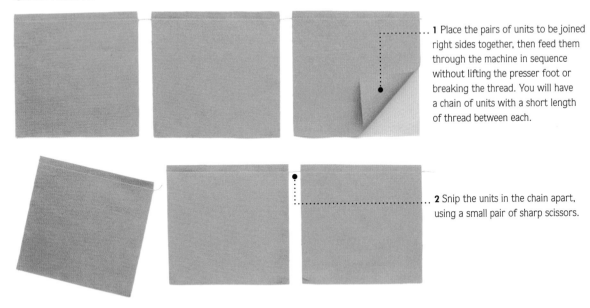

1 Place the pairs of units to be joined right sides together, then feed them through the machine in sequence without lifting the presser foot or breaking the thread. You will have a chain of units with a short length of thread between each.

2 Snip the units in the chain apart, using a small pair of sharp scissors.

▶▶SEWING INTERSECTING SEAMS

When sewing together any two pieces of patchwork, it is important to match the seams so that they align perfectly with the seams on the adjoining piece. By pressing the seams in opposite directions and fitting them into one another, known as nesting, you can create smooth, accurate seams without any gaps or misalignments.

MATCHING STRAIGHT SEAMS

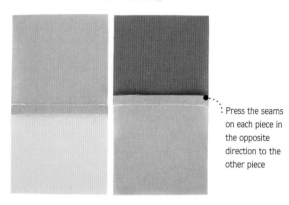

Press the seams on each piece in the opposite direction to the other piece

1 After piecing plain squares or rectangles together, press the seams on each strip to be joined in the opposite direction to the seams on the strip it will be joined to.

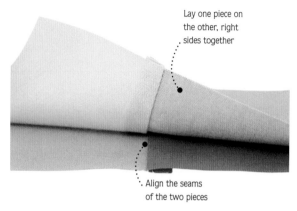

Lay one piece on the other, right sides together

Align the seams of the two pieces

2 Place the pieces right sides together, taking care to align the seams.

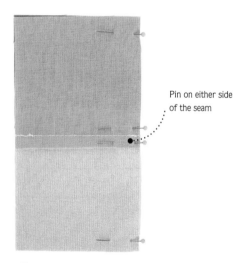

Pin on either side of the seam

3 Nest the seams by running your finger over the spot where all four pieces of fabric meet, to feel for any gaps. Ensure that opposite seams butt right up against one another smoothly. Carefully pin on either side of the nested seams. If there are multiple joins along the two pieces, match each point, then work outwards from each pinned seam, towards the ends.

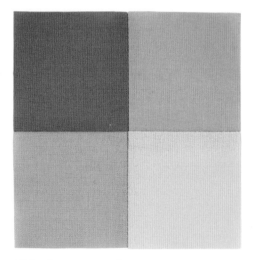

4 Using the same seam allowance you used to join the pieces, sew through the layers, taking care when sewing over the matched seams. Remove the pins as you work. Open out and press the finished item.

MATCHING SEAMS WITH POINTS

When joining pieces of patchwork that have points, it is important
to match the seams correctly, so as not to lose the points in the seam.

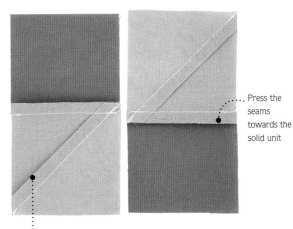

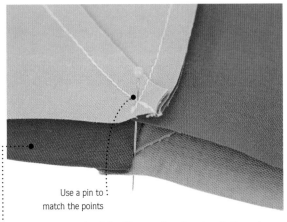

Press the
seams
towards the
solid unit

Use a pin to
match the points

1 Press the seams on the two pieces to be
joined in opposite directions, ideally away
from the piece with the point.

2 Place the two units right sides together. Insert a pin through
the top piece, right at the end of the point. Insert the pin
straight down through the bottom piece, at the tip of the point.

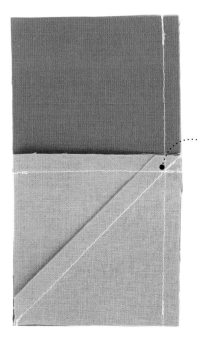

The stitching
should pass right
over the point

3 Nest the seam by running your finger over the
spot where all the pieces of fabric meet to feel for
any gaps. Carefully pin on either side of the seam
to be matched, then continue pinning, working
outwards. Sew along the seam using the same
seam allowance previously used to join the pieces.
Remove the pins as you work.

4 Open out the piece and press.

⧗▶ TRIANGLES

Triangles form the basis of many patchwork units and, after squares and rectangles, are the next easiest and most versatile to work with. They can be combined with other triangle units or with plain units to create a wide range of blocks. Triangle units also make a wonderful impact when used in sashings and borders.

MAKING A PAIR OF HALF-SQUARE TRIANGLES

While a half-square triangle, which is a square made of two right-angled triangles, can be made by sewing two triangles together, a faster way is to start with two squares and use the method below.

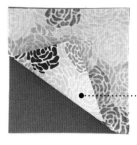

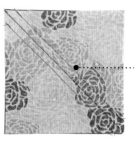

1 Cut two squares, each 2.2cm (⅞in) larger than the desired finished size and place them right sides together, with the lighter colour on top.

2 Using a pencil, mark a diagonal line in one direction across the wrong side of the lighter-coloured square.

3 Pin, then machine stitch along each side of the marked line, stitching 6mm (¼in) from the line.

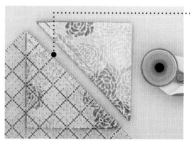

4 Using a rotary cutter or scissors, cut along the pencil line.

5 Open out the pieces of fabric and press the seams, usually towards the darker fabric, to make two identical half-square triangles.

Trim the "dog ear" points at each end of the seam

MAKING MULTIPLE HALF-SQUARE TRIANGLES FROM STRIPS

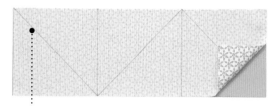

1 Start by cutting fabric strips that are the desired width plus 2.2cm (⅞in). Place them right sides together and mark squares on the wrong side of the lighter fabric. Draw a diagonal line across each square, alternating the direction of the line in each square.

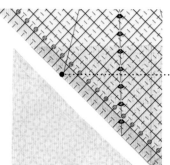

2 Sew a 6mm (¼in) seam on each side of the marked diagonal lines. Cut along the marked diagonal and vertical lines to separate the half-square triangles. Press the seams towards the darker fabric.

MAKING MULTIPLE HALF-SQUARE TRIANGLES FROM LARGE PIECES

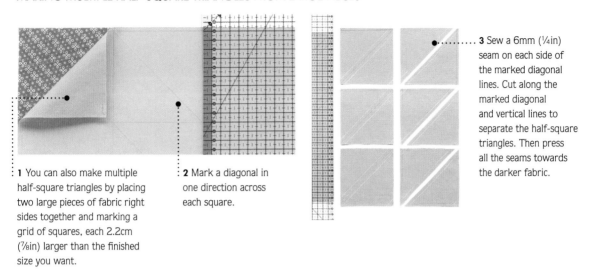

1 You can also make multiple half-square triangles by placing two large pieces of fabric right sides together and marking a grid of squares, each 2.2cm (⅞in) larger than the finished size you want.

2 Mark a diagonal in one direction across each square.

3 Sew a 6mm (¼in) seam on each side of the marked diagonal lines. Cut along the marked diagonal and vertical lines to separate the half-square triangles. Then press all the seams towards the darker fabric.

MAKING A PAIR OF QUARTER-SQUARE TRIANGLES

Quarter-square triangles can be quickly made using the technique below. Start by making two half-square triangles using one of the techniques already described opposite and above. Begin with two squares each 2.75cm (1⅜in) larger than the desired finished size.

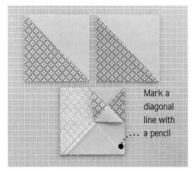

Mark a diagonal line with a pencil

1 Place the two half-square triangles right sides together, with the seams aligned and the contrasting fabrics face to face.

2 Using a pencil, mark a diagonal line from corner to corner in the opposite direction from the seamline that is on top. Sew a 6mm (¼in) seam either side of the marked line.

WRONG SIDE

RIGHT SIDE

3 Cut the units apart along the marked diagonal lines and press.

JOINING PIECED AND PLAIN UNITS

1 Place one half-square triangle (the pieced unit) and one plain unit right sides together. Sew together, as shown, leaving a 6mm (¼in) seam allowance. On the right side, the corner of the half-square triangle will disappear in the seam allowance 6mm (¼in) from the raw edge. Repeat for the other pieced and plain unit.

2 Combining two pairs of joined pieced and plain units, as shown, will accommodate the seam allowances and their corners will meet exactly in the centre of the four units.

⏩▶EQUILATERAL TRIANGLES

Joining equilateral triangles requires slightly off setting each triangle using the "dog ears" left by the previous seam. This will ensure that the finished row is straight and even.

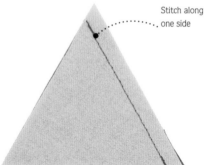

Stitch along one side

1 Using a rotary cutter and quilter's ruler with 60-degree guides, cut out your triangles.

2 Align two of the triangles, right sides together, and carefully stitch along one side.

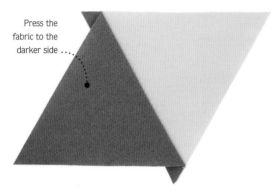

Press the fabric to the darker side

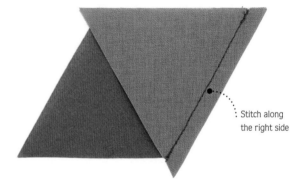

Stitch along the right side

3 Unfold and press the seam allowances towards the darker fabric.

4 Using the ears from the first two triangles as a guide, align the third triangle and pin. Carefully stitch along the edge of the triangles.

Unfold and press

5 Unfold and press. Repeat Steps 2–4 adding as many triangles as your design requires.

▶▶FLYING GEESE

Flying geese blocks are an easily adaptable and versatile design. They can be added to the borders of blocks to add more visual interest or can be used as a block on their own. They are often used to make star points in blocks.

1 Cut a rectangle 1.2cm (½in) both wider and longer than the required finished size of your unit. Cut two squares of the same height and width as the short side of the rectangle. Draw a diagonal line from corner to corner on the wrong side of the squares.

2 Pin the square to the left side of the rectangle, right sides together, with the diagonal line positioned as shown. Carefully stitch along the line.

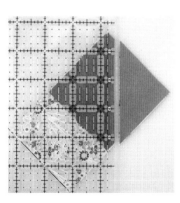

3 Using your quilter's ruler, trim off the excess fabric from the corner, leaving a 6mm (¼in) seam allowance. Align your ruler with the stitching line, as shown.

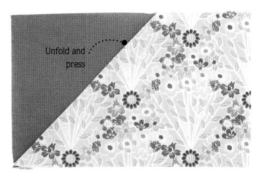

Unfold and press

4 Unfold and press the unit.

Sew through the line

5 Repeat the process on the right side of the rectangle, positioning the second square as shown. Pin in place and sew along the line.

Trim the excess and press

6 Trim away the excess as in Step 3 and press the seams open.

⫸▶ TRIANGLE CORNERS

Triangle corners are made the same way as Flying geese (see p.67), but four corners are added around a square instead of two to a rectangle. This can be a good method of adding a border around a completed block, to tilt it on its point.

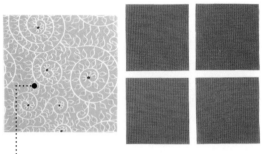

1 Cut one large square from a fabric to the required size. Cut four squares, each half the size of the larger square, plus 6mm (¼in) extra, from another fabric. Here we have used a 9cm (3½in) large square and four 5.1cm (2in) small squares.

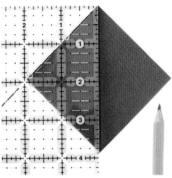
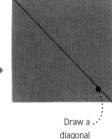

Draw a diagonal line across the square

2 Draw diagonal lines on the wrong side of the smaller squares, as shown.

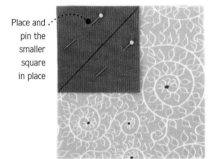

Place and pin the smaller square in place

3 Place and pin the smaller square on the upper left corner of the larger square with the diagonal line as shown.

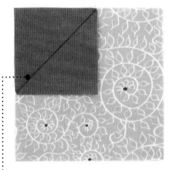

4 Carefully stitch through the diagonal line of the smaller square.

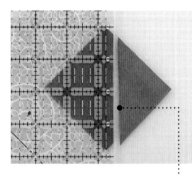

5 Using a rotary cutter and quilter's ruler, trim off the excess fabric, leaving a 6mm (¼in) seam allowance.

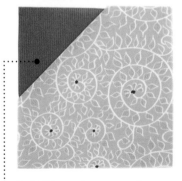

6 Unfold the smaller square and press into position.

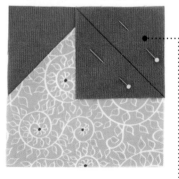

7 Repeat the process on the remaining three corners, working clockwise.

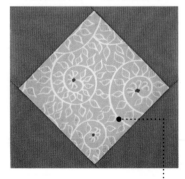

8 With the right side facing up, press flat.

▶ SEWING TRIANGLES TO SQUARES

Attaching triangles to squares can be difficult, especially as the edges of the triangle may be cut on the bias. Follow Steps 2–4 below to attach one triangle to a square, but if you'd like to add them all around a square to create a block, complete the entire sequence.

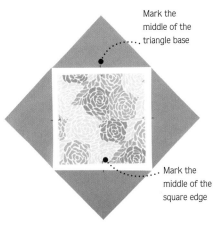

Mark the middle of the triangle base

Mark the middle of the square edge

1 Cut a square of your required size, then cut triangles with a long side of the same width, plus 6mm (¼in) extra. Make marks in the centre of all four sides of the square and the longest edge of each of the triangles.

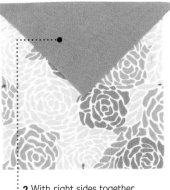

2 With right sides together, place a triangle along the top edge of the square, aligning the centre points. Make sure the triangle is centred along the edge so the side points overhang by equal amounts.

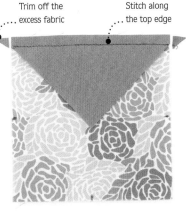

Trim off the excess fabric

Stitch along the top edge

3 Carefully stitch along the top edge using a 6mm (¼in) seam allowance. Trim off the excess fabric on the sides to square up the block.

Unfold the triangle and press

4 Unfold the triangle and press the seam towards the square.

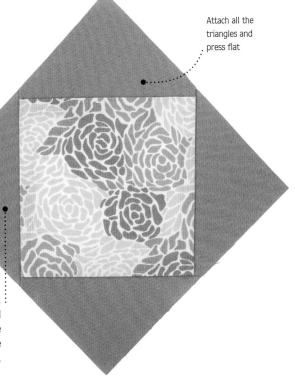

Attach all the triangles and press flat

5 Repeat the process, working clockwise, until all four sides of the centre square have a triangle attached. Press flat.

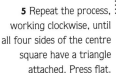

Star designs make up the largest group of patchwork patterns. They range from simple four-patch blocks to highly elaborate blocks with multiple star points.

Making them combines many techniques. The following patterns are the starting points for numerous variations.

SINGLE STAR: DOUBLE FOUR-PATCH

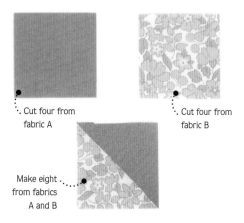

`·.` Cut four from fabric A

`·.` Cut four from fabric B

Make eight `·.....` from fabrics A and B

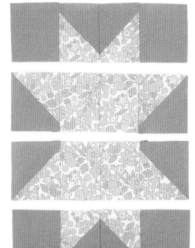

2 Following the layout and with right sides together, stitch the squares and half-square triangles together in rows of four, leaving a 6mm (¼in) seam allowance.

1 Divide the size of the finished block by four. Add seam allowances. Cut and make eight half-square triangles from fabrics A and B (see p.64). Cut an additional four squares each of fabric A and fabric B.

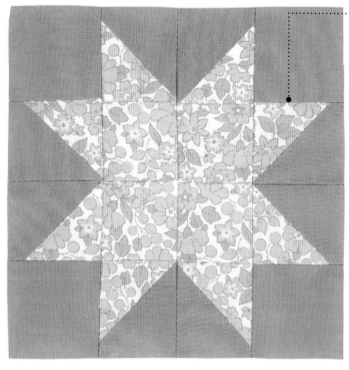

3 With right sides together, stitch the rows together, matching the seams and leaving a 6mm (¼in) seam allowance.

FRIENDSHIP STAR: NINE-PATCH

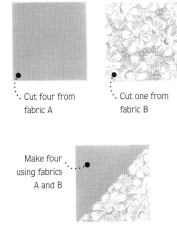

Cut four from fabric A

Cut one from fabric B

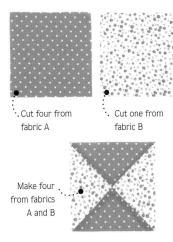

Make four using fabrics A and B

1 Divide the size of the finished block by three. Add seam allowances. Cut four squares from fabric A and one square from fabric B. Make four half-square triangles from fabrics A and B (see p.64).

2 Following the layout and with right sides together, stitch the squares and half-square triangles together in rows of three, leaving a 6mm (¼in) seam allowance.

3 With right sides together, stitch the rows together, matching the seams and leaving a 6mm (¼in) seam allowance.

OHIO STAR: NINE-PATCH WITH QUARTER-SQUARE TRIANGLES

Cut four from fabric A

Cut one from fabric B

Make four from fabrics A and B

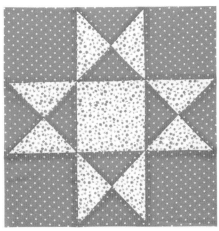

1 Divide the size of the finished block by three. Add seam allowances. Cut four squares from fabric A and one square from fabric B. Make four quarter-square triangles from fabrics A and B (see p.65).

2 Following the layout and with right sides together, stitch the squares and quarter-square triangles together in rows of three, leaving a 6mm (¼in) seam allowance.

3 With right sides together, stitch the rows together, matching the seams and leaving a 6mm (¼in) seam allowance.

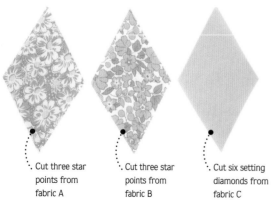

.'. Cut three star
points from
fabric A

.'. Cut three star
points from
fabric B

.'. Cut six setting
diamonds from
fabric C

1 Cut 12 60-degree-angle diamonds, as above. Those
in fabrics A and B will be the points of the star, and
those in fabric C will be the setting diamonds. Add
a seam allowance all around each diamond.

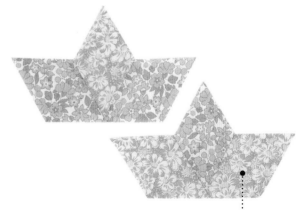

2 With right sides together, stitch the three star
points together in units of three, alternating
the fabrics as above.

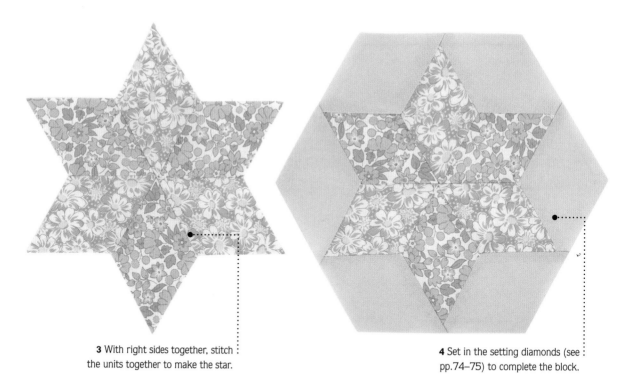

3 With right sides together, stitch
the units together to make the star.

4 Set in the setting diamonds (see
pp.74–75) to complete the block.

EIGHT-POINT STAR: 45-DEGREE ANGLES

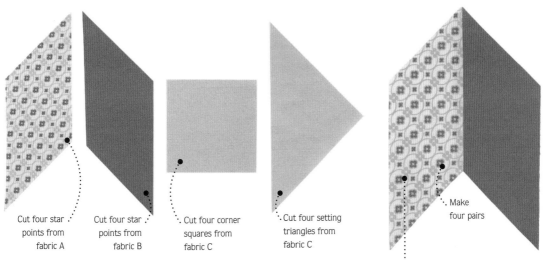

Cut four star points from fabric A

Cut four star points from fabric B

Cut four corner squares from fabric C

Cut four setting triangles from fabric C

Make four pairs

1 Make templates to the desired size for the points of the star, the corner squares, and the setting triangles. Cut four 45-degree-angle diamonds (see p.37) each from fabrics A and B for the points of the star, and four corner squares (see p.35) and four setting triangles (see p.37) from fabric C.

2 With right sides together, stitch the star points together in four identical pairs, using one fabric A point and one fabric B point for each pair.

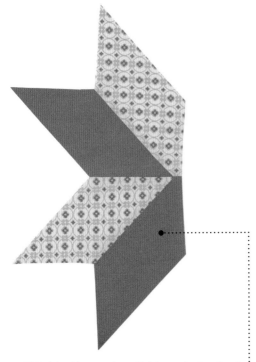

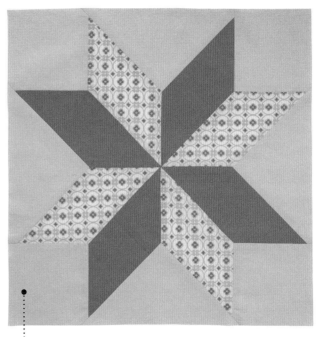

3 With right sides together, stitch two pairs together to make half the star, repeat to make the other half, then stitch the two halves together to complete the star.

4 Set in the setting triangles, then set in the corner squares (see pp.74–75) to complete the block.

⏵▶ SET-IN SEAMS

Most patchwork involves joining straight seams, but in some cases you will need to join three pieces of fabric into one corner. This is called a set-in seam or a Y-seam.

You will need to measure, mark, and stitch carefully, starting and finishing the distance of your seam allowance away from each set-in corner.

SETTING IN BY HAND

1 Diamonds and triangles sometimes meet at oblique angles. Setting a piece into the resulting space needs careful pinning and sewing. Here, a square is set in the space between two diamond shapes. Cut the square to size and mark 6mm (¼in) seamlines. Mark the starting and finishing points 6mm (¼in) from the edges.

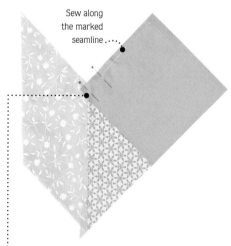

Sew along the marked seamline

2 Match one corner of the square to the inner point on the first diamond and pin, right sides together. Match the outer point and pin. Pin the edges together along the seamline. Sew along the marked seamline from the outer point to the inner, removing pins as you work. Take a few small backstitches into the seam at the inner corner, avoiding the seam allowance. Make sure not to cut the thread.

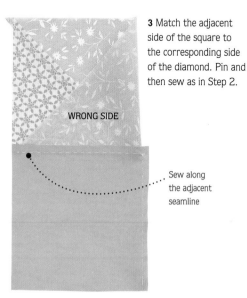

WRONG SIDE

Sew along the adjacent seamline

3 Match the adjacent side of the square to the corresponding side of the diamond. Pin and then sew as in Step 2.

4 Press the seam allowances on the square towards the two diamonds.

SETTING IN BY MACHINE

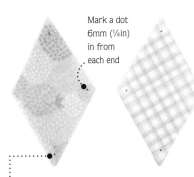

Mark a dot 6mm (¼in) in from each end

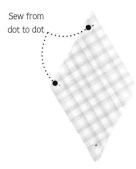

Sew from dot to dot

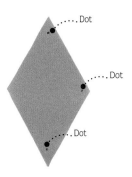

Dot

Dot

Dot

1 Using a light pencil or water-soluble marker, mark a dot 6mm (¼in) in from each end of the two pieces that are to be joined first. This marks the point where you start and finish stitching. Do not stitch to the very end of the seam.

2 Place the shapes right sides together and sew from dot to dot, back stitching at each end. Do not overshoot the dots. Press the seam towards the darker fabric.

3 On the wrong side of the piece that is to be set in, mark a dot 6mm (¼in) in at the three set-in corners of the piece.

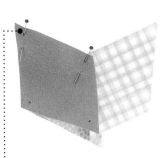

WRONG SIDE AFTER STITCHING

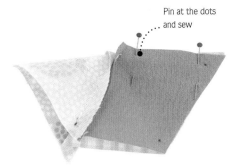

Pin at the dots and sew

4 Match the middle marked corner of the piece that is to be set in with the corresponding dot on one of the two pieces that have already been stitched together. Pin the seam at each end and sew from the inside corner to the outer dot.

5 Match the outer dot on the second side of the piece that is to be set in with the outer dot on the free edge of the other piece. Pin them together at the dot and sew, again stitching from the inside corner to the outer dot.

6 Press the seams flat in one direction. Snip off the corners.

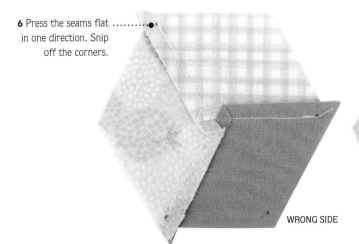

WRONG SIDE

RIGHT SIDE

The way quilt blocks are arranged in a finished top is called the set, or setting. The following section can give only an outline of the virtually infinite possibilities for putting blocks together. The way to work out the best setting for a quilt is to lay out all of the blocks and view them from a distance.

QUILT LAYOUTS

Many quilt blocks, even fairly simple ones, can create interesting secondary patterns when they are joined, and rotating or reversing blocks makes a quilt look entirely different.

STRAIGHT SETS

The simplest sets are rows of repeating blocks stitched together edge to edge, referred to as "straight set".

ALTERNATING PIECED AND PLAIN

Alternating a pieced block with a plain block means there are fewer blocks to put together. It allows for large, open areas, perfect for showcasing elaborate quilting.

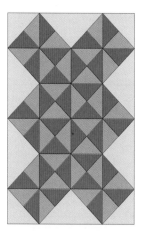

ON POINT: SOLID SET

Blocks can be set "on point" (turned on the diagonal), with setting triangles around the edges and at each corner.

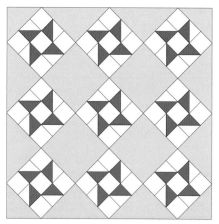

ON POINT: ALTERNATING PIECED AND PLAIN BLOCKS

This setting needs plain blocks between the pieced blocks as well as triangles added to each corner and along each side to fill the edges.

LIGHT AND DARK

BARN RAISING

STRAIGHT FURROW

Log cabin

There are so many possible sets for log cabin designs that each version has its own name. The examples above all have the same number of identical log cabin blocks. In each case, the way each block is turned determines the final overall effect.

FRAME SETTINGS

STRIPPY SET

ROTATING BLOCKS

Also known as medallion settings, these have a central block, sometimes an elaborate appliqué, surrounded by several borders of various widths, some pieced, some plain. The centre can be set square or on point as here.

When blocks are arranged vertically, a strippy set results. The first strippy quilts were usually simple strips of fabric joined to make the width of a quilt, but beautiful strippy quilts can be made from pieced blocks, too.

This setting creates new patterns once several blocks are set, particularly with asymmetrical patterns.

Sashing is strips of fabric placed between blocks to frame them. Sampler quilts and star blocks usually have sashing to give each block the chance to shine. The width of the sashing is flexible: try out different widths before you cut the strips. Plain or pieced squares (known as setting squares or cornerstones) can be placed at the corners of a block to make the pattern even more interesting.

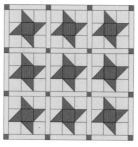

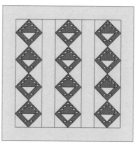

Straight-set simple continuous sashing Each block in this piece is framed by straight-set simple sashing.

Straight-set sashing with setting squares Adding a square in each corner between the blocks creates more pattern. The setting squares can also be pieced; simple pinwheel, four-patch, and nine-patch designs work well.

Vertical or horizontal set sashing Blocks can be assembled in rows with the sashing between them running vertically or horizontally.

Diagonal set (on point) with sashing Blocks set on point can be framed by sashing and assembled in strips with extra triangles added around the edges to give a chevron effect.

SIMPLE CONTINUOUS SASHING

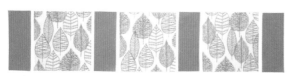

1 Cut sashing strips to the desired width plus a 1.2cm (½in) seam allowance, and to the same length as one side of the blocks.

2 With right sides together and leaving a 6mm (¼in) seam allowance, alternate strips and blocks to make a row. Press the seams towards the strips. Repeat to make as many rows as needed.

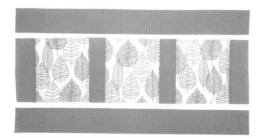

3 Cut two more sashing strips to the desired width plus a 1.2cm (½in) seam allowance, and the same length as the joined row.

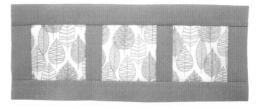

4 With right sides together and leaving a 6mm (¼in) seam allowance, sew the two strips either side of the row. Press the seams towards the sashing. Continue alternating sashing strips and rows of blocks with strips until the quilt top is the required size.

SASHING WITH SETTING SQUARES

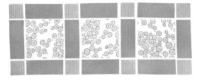

1 Repeat Steps 1 and 2 of Simple continuous sashing (opposite) to make a row of blocks. For the sashing, cut strips the same length as the width of a block, and setting squares the same width as the strips.

2 With right sides together and leaving a 6mm (¼in) seam allowance, alternate squares and strips to make two long sashing strips.

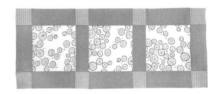

3 With right sides together and leaving a 6mm (¼in) seam allowance, machine stitch the long sashing strips along the top and bottom edges of the row of blocks. Ensure that the corners of the blocks and the setting squares match up. Continue alternating rows of sashing strips and blocks until the quilt is the required size.

TILTED BLOCK SETTING

1 First make the central block, then frame it with a wide border made from four pieces of sashing, as shown left.

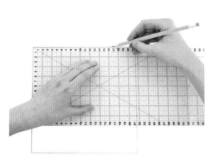

2 Create a template for the block by measuring and marking its size on tracing paper, adding 1.2cm (½in) seam allowances.

3 Centre the template on top of the block that was made in Step 1, then angle the template to the desired tilt.

4 In order to be able to tilt subsequent blocks at the same angle, use a ruler and pencil to mark the outline of the central block on the template.

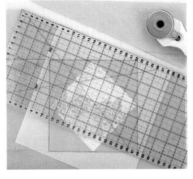

5 Cut away the fabric around the template. To reuse the template, ensure that all central blocks in the project align with the block marked on the template.

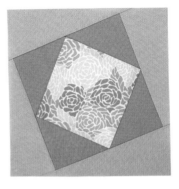

6 When the finished block is placed so its outside edges are perpendicular, the central block will be tilted.

The outside edges of most quilts are finished with strips that make up the border. This frames the piece and protects the edges. Borders can be single or multiple, wide or narrow, pieced or plain. Whatever type you choose, the border should complement and enhance the overall design of the quilt. If possible, strips should be cut along the lengthways grain, in one long piece and with the selvedges removed. Never cut borders on the bias.

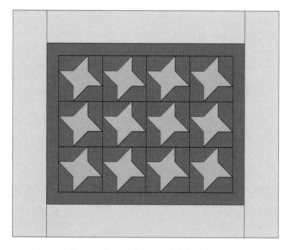

Straight borders Adding a plain, straight border is an easy-to-make, popular choice. When made from plain fabric, it gives an uncluttered look and is especially effective when framing a complex design.

Mitred borders More complex than straight borders, well-executed mitred borders look very professional and neat. The corners are stitched at a 45-degree angle to the sides of the quilt.

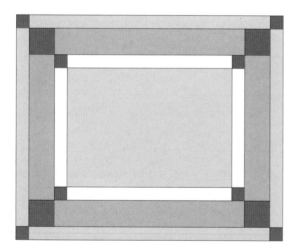

Multiple borders with setting squares You can add several borders to a quilt, together with setting squares in the corners. The effect is a little like a series of "retreating" picture frames.

Pieced inner border with straight outer border Another variation on multiple borders uses a straight outer border framing an inner border made of pieced patchwork.

MAKING STRAIGHT BORDERS

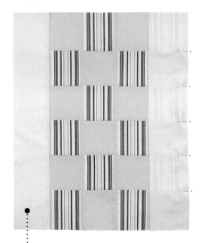

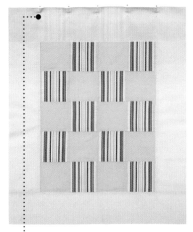

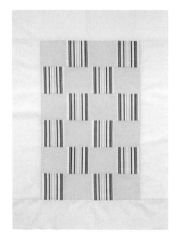

1 Cut or piece two strips of the desired width, plus 1.2cm (½in) for seam allowances, and the same length as the sides of the quilt. Mark the centre of each strip and of the sides of the quilt. Pin the strips to the quilt, right sides together and matching the marks. Sew together, leaving a 6mm (¼in) seam allowance.

2 Press the seams towards the border strips. Measure the top and bottom edges of the quilt plus borders, and cut two strips to that length. Mark the centre of each strip and of the top and bottom edges, as in Step 1. Pin with right sides together, matching the marks. Sew together, leaving a 6mm (¼in) seam allowance. Press the seams towards the border strips.

3 The quilt top is now completed and ready to be quilted (see pp.130–133, 134–137).

JOINING STRIPS TO MAKE A BORDER

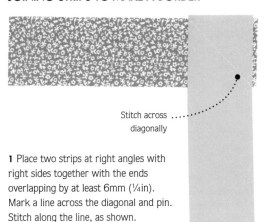

Stitch across .....
diagonally

Trim the edges .....
to even them up

1 Place two strips at right angles with right sides together with the ends overlapping by at least 6mm (¼in). Mark a line across the diagonal and pin. Stitch along the line, as shown.

2 Trim the seam to 6mm (¼in), then open out the joined strips to the right side. Trim the edges of the strip, if needed. Press the seam to one side.

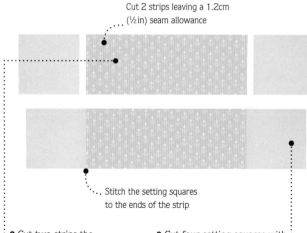

Cut 2 strips leaving a 1.2cm (½in) seam allowance

Stitch the setting squares to the ends of the strip

1 Follow Step 1 of Making straight borders (see p.81) to add a border to the piece on either side. Press the seams towards the borders.

2 Cut two strips the same length as the top and bottom edges of the quilt without the borders, plus a 1.2cm (½in) seam allowance.

3 Cut four setting squares with sides the width of the borders. With right sides together, sew a square to each end of the strips. Press the seams towards the centre.

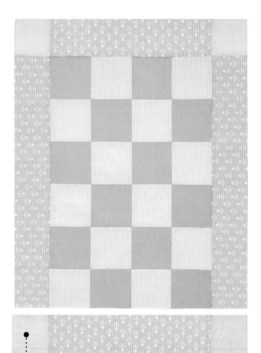

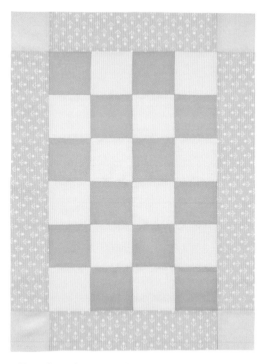

4 With right sides together, sew the pieced strips to the top and bottom edges of the quilt. Press the seams towards the border.

5 The quilt top is now completed and ready to be quilted (see pp.130–133, 134–137).

MAKING A MITRED BORDER

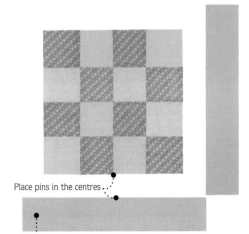

Place pins in the centres

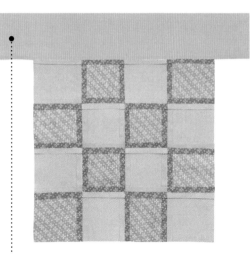

1 Square up the quilt top. Cut the border strips to the desired width plus 1.2cm (½in) for seam allowances. Measure the length of the quilt top sides, then add two times the width of the border, plus 15.5cm (6in) to calculate the length.

2 Place a pin in the centre of each side of the quilt top and each border. Aligning the centre pins, position the borders right side together with the corresponding side and pin in place. Position a pin 6mm (¼in) from each corner to mark your starting and stopping points for stitching.

3 Join the border strips to all sides of the quilt, leaving a 6mm (¼in) seam allowance. Do not stitch into adjoining border strips. Press the seams towards the borders.

MULTIPLE MITRED BORDERS

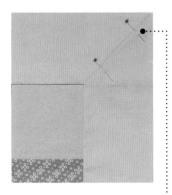

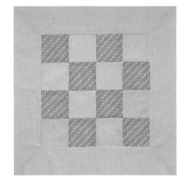

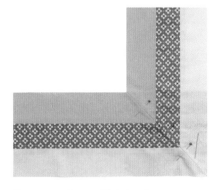

4 Place the quilt right side up on a flat surface and fold under the ends of each strip at a 45-degree angle. Pin the folds in place from the right side, ensuring that the angle is correct. Press the folds and remove the pins.

5 Working from the wrong side, re-pin the mitre along the pressed fold. Tack in place if desired. Hand stitch the fold together from the quilt edge to the outside corner. Trim the seam allowance and press it open. Repeat to mitre all corners.

If you are using multiple borders, join them together in straight rows and attach them to the quilt top in one go. Mitre the corners as in Steps 4 and 5, making sure you match the borders through the mitre.

⚞▶CURVES

Patchwork patterns based on curves are less common than those with straight seams, which are easy to cut and stitch. But although curves can be fiddly, they give more options and, with careful preparation at every stage from template making to cutting and pinning, they are straightforward to sew. Many people find curves easier to work by hand, but it is not difficult to machine stitch them.

SEWING CURVED SEAMS BY HAND

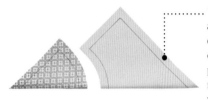

1 Mark the seamlines and any registration marks, especially the centre point, on the wrong side of each piece. If the centre isn't marked on the pattern, fold each piece in half, fingerpress it at the centre seamline, and use the crease as the centre mark.

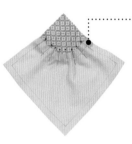

2 Place the smaller convex piece right sides together on the concave one, aligning the centre points. Pin the centre point through both pieces. Pin the end points of the marked seamline. Then pin along the seamline every 1cm (⅜in) or so, manipulating the fabric to eliminate creases.

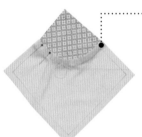

3 Take out the pin at one end and take the needle through the matching points. You may use a double backstitched loop (see p.40) in the seamline to secure the thread. Do not sew into the seam allowance. Take several short running stitches along the seamline, then pull the needle through. Repeat along the length of the seam, removing pins as you work. Secure the seam further by making a small back stitch each time you bring the needle through.

4 Check the back to make sure your stitching is on the line on both sides and stop at the matching point at the end. Do not sew into the seam allowance, but use a double backstitched loop to secure the thread. Do not clip the seam allowance. Press the seam towards the convex piece. If your stitching is accurate, the piece will lie flat.

SEWING CURVED SEAMS BY MACHINE

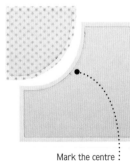

Mark the centre point of the curve

1 Make templates and mark the centre of the curve on each one. Cut out the fabric pieces, adding a 6mm (¼in) seam allowance. Centre the templates on the wrong side of your fabric pieces, draw around them to mark the seam allowances, then mark the centre point of the curve on the fabric pieces.

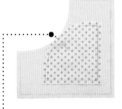

2 Pin the two fabric pieces together at the centre point on the seam allowance, then pin at each end. Pin along the edge to stabilize the curve.

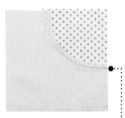

3 Stitch along the marked curve without stretching or pulling. Remove the pins as you sew. Press the seam towards the convex piece. It should lie flat without being clipped.

REDUCING SEAM BULK

Sometimes you may need to reduce the bulk in curved seams to help your patchwork lie flat. This is usually used on 3-dimensional objects.

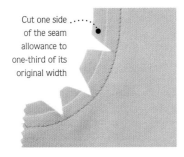

Cut one side of the seam allowance to one-third of its original width

Reducing bulk on an inner curve Layer the seam by cutting along one side of the seam allowance to reduce it to one-third of its original width. Then cut out V notches to reduce the bulk. Do not cut through the stitching.

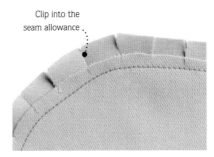

Clip into the seam allowance

Reducing bulk on an outer curve Layer the seam and clip through the seam allowances to reduce bulk.

FANS

1 Transfer the outlines to card or template plastic and cut out the shapes. Make two sets of templates – set 1 for the cutting lines, and set 2 with the seam allowances trimmed off the curved edges for the stitching line.

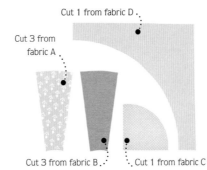

Cut 1 from fabric D

Cut 3 from fabric A

Cut 3 from fabric B

Cut 1 from fabric C

2 For a six-blade fan, cut three blades each from fabrics A and B. Cut a small corner piece from fabric C and a background from fabric D.

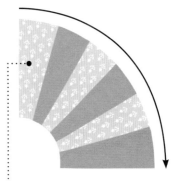

3 Join the fan blade pieces, alternating the colours and taking a 6mm (¼in) seam allowance. Press the blades in the same direction.

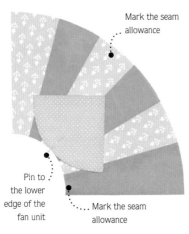

Mark the seam allowance

Pin to the lower edge of the fan unit

Mark the seam allowance

4 Mark the seam allowances on the top and bottom edges of the fan unit.

5 Mark the seam allowance on the small corner piece and pin it to the lower edge of the fan unit. Join them as in Steps 5 and 6 of Drunkard's path (see pp.86–87). Press towards the fan.

6 Mark the seam allowance on the background piece and pin the background piece to the upper edge of the fan unit. Join them as before. Press towards the background.

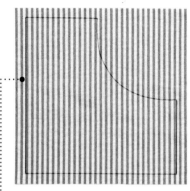

Trace around the
set 1 template

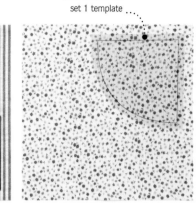

1 Make two sets of templates from card or plastic – set 1 for the cutting lines, and set 2 with the seam allowances trimmed off the curved edges for the stitching line. Place the registration marks precisely on both sets.

2 Trace the larger outlines onto the wrong side of the chosen fabrics. Make sure the registration marks are transferred accurately.

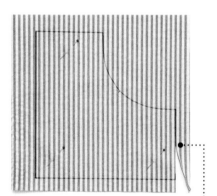

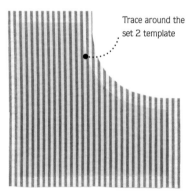

Trace around the
set 2 template

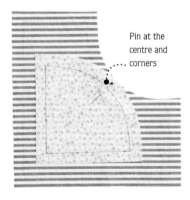

Pin at the
centre and
corners

3 Cut out the shapes. If you are using scissors, cut around the curve, not into it. If you prefer to cut with rotary equipment, use the smallest size blade (25mm/1in) and a perfectly smooth cutting mat for best results.

4 Separate the cut-out shapes and, using the set 2 templates, trace the seamlines and registration marks onto the wrong side of each fabric piece.

5 Pin one of each shape and fabric right sides together, with the convex piece on top of the concave one. Match and pin the centre marks first, then pin the corners.

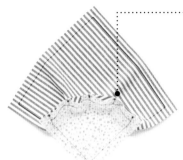

6 Place pins in between, every 1cm (⅜in) or so, matching the seamlines on both pieces as necessary and using your fingers and thumbs to manipulate and ease the fabric to eliminate uneven distribution.

Seam stitched 6mm (¼in) from the edge

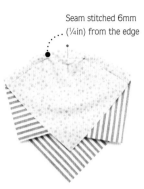

7 Slowly stitch along the seamlines marked on the curved seam of each piece, removing pins as you sew. If you pin in advance, you can chain piece these units.

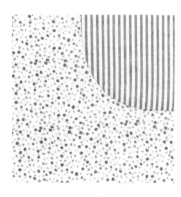

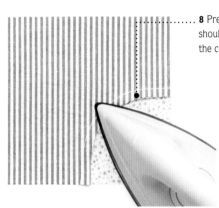

8 Press the seams. There should be no need to clip the curves.

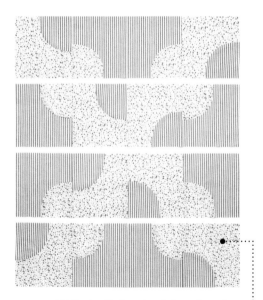

9 Following the layout and alternating colours, combine the units in four rows of four. Press the seams in opposite directions on alternate rows.

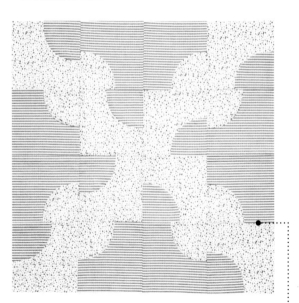

10 Join the rows, matching the seams carefully. Press.

⥤▶ ENGLISH PAPER PIECING

This is a traditional method for making a quilt of mosaic shapes. The fabric pieces – hexagons, honeycombs, diamonds, and triangles, all of which have at least two bias edges – are tacked to pre-cut paper templates the size of the finished element. The technique is usually done by hand. The backing papers can be cut from virtually any heavy paper, but freezer paper can be ironed on quickly and is easy to remove.

BASIC PAPER-PIECING TECHNIQUE

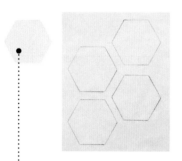

1 Unless you are using pre-cut paper shapes, make a template. Draw around it to make the necessary number of shapes. Using paper scissors, carefully cut out the backing papers.

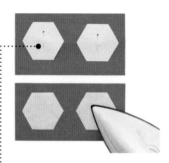

2 Pin a plain-paper shape or iron a freezer-paper shape (paper side up) to the wrong side of the fabric. Leave enough space for seam allowances.

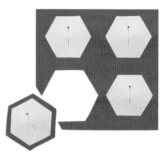

3 Cut out each shape from fabric, leaving a 6mm (¼in) seam allowance all around. You can use scissors or a rotary cutter, but take care to keep at least one side of the shape along the straight grain of the fabric.

Fold and tack the seam allowance

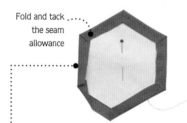

4 Turn the seam allowance to the wrong side over the edge of the paper shape. Fold the seam allowance in each corner neatly and place a few tacking stitches through the wax paper and fabric, holding it securely in place.

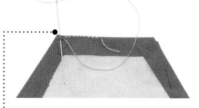

5 To join patches into units, place two shapes right sides together. Make a backstitched loop (see p.40), and oversew to the corner as close to the fold as possible. Do not sew through the backing papers.

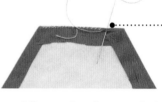

6 Oversew along the same edge to the opposite corner, again taking small stitches. When you reach the corner, backstitch in the opposite direction for 6mm (¼in).

7 Continue adding shapes until complete. If you wish to reuse papers, you can remove them once all the shapes adjoining a particular piece have been added by clipping the tacking stitches and carefully pulling the paper out.

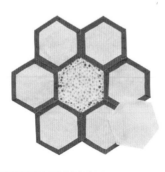

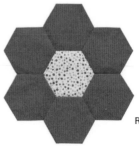

RIGHT SIDE

SETTING IN HEXAGONS

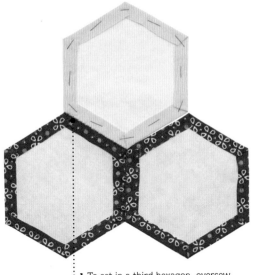

1 To set in a third hexagon, oversew one side of the seam, starting at the centre point.

2 Align the second sides to be joined at their outer points, folding back the pieces as necessary, and stitch as before.

NEAT FOLDS

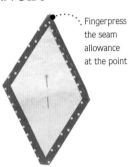

Fingerpress the seam allowance at the point

1 To make a neat fold at the sharp points when tacking diamonds and triangles, start sewing in the middle of one side. When you reach the point, fingerpress the extended seam allowance.

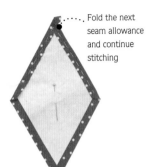

Fold the next seam allowance and continue stitching

2 Fold over the allowance from the next side neatly. Take a stitch through the fold and continue. Do not trim off the fabric extensions.

NEAT JOINS

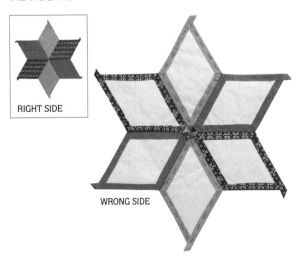

RIGHT SIDE

WRONG SIDE

To make a neat join when you sew pieces together, fold the extension to the side so that you don't stitch through it. Where several come together, the unstitched extensions will form a spiral around their meeting point and lie flat.

➤▶ STRIP PIECING

Strip piecing is a good way to build blocks quickly. In principle, several long strips are joined – or pieced – and then cut apart before being stitched together again in a different sequence. It is the method by which many blocks can be made, including Log cabin (see pp.92–93) and Seminole patchwork (see pp.99–101).

STRIP-PIECED BLOCKS: RAIL FENCE

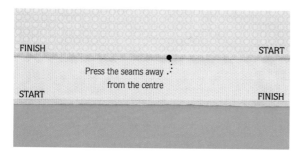

FINISH   START

Press the seams away
from the centre

START   FINISH

1 Cut three strips of equal width from three contrasting fabrics. With right sides together, stitch them lengthways, leaving a 6mm (¼in) seam allowance. To prevent the pieced strip from bowing, join strips 1 and 2, then reverse the direction of sewing to add strip 3. Press the seams to one side, away from the centre.

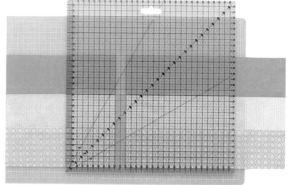

2 Using a rotary cutter and quilter's ruler, measure the width of the pieced strip and cut across it to make squares the same size on each side as this measurement.

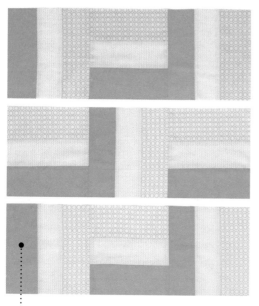

3 Following the layout, arrange the squares in rows of three. With right sides together, join the squares to make three rows, leaving a 6mm (¼in) seam allowance. Press, alternating the direction in each row.

4 With right sides together, join the rows, matching the seams and leaving a 6mm (¼in) seam allowance.

▶ STRING PIECING

String piecing is similar to strip piecing, but the lengths of fabric are not necessarily straight strips and are referred to as "strings". The string-pieced blocks can be combined to make larger units.

If using a paper foundation block for Method 2, use a stitch length of around 1.5 to perforate the paper making it easier to remove.

METHOD 1

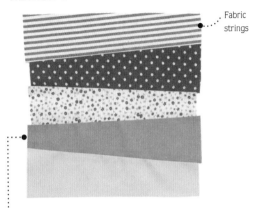

Fabric strings

1 Select "strings" of fabric with plenty of colour and pattern contrast. With right sides together, stitch them together lengthways, leaving a 6mm (¼in) seam allowance. Alternate the angle as you add each piece and alternate the direction of stitching each time to prevent bowing.

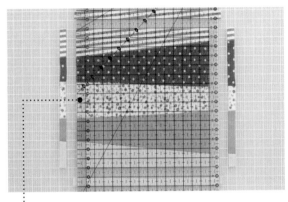

2 Press the seams to one side. Using a rotary cutter and quilter's ruler, trim the piece to the desired size and shape.

METHOD 2

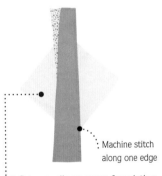

Machine stitch along one edge

Trim the edges

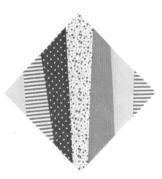

1 Cut a muslin or paper foundation block, plus seam allowances. Place the first string right side up in the centre of the block and lay the second string right side down on top. Make sure both strings are longer than the block at its widest point. Machine stitch along one edge of the strips through all layers. Flip the joined pieces open and press.

2 Turn the foundation block, then add a new string, right side down, to the free edge of the first string. Flip the joined pieces open and press.

3 Continue to add strings, flip, press, and stitch, until the foundation block is covered. Trim the edges level with the foundation. If you have used a paper foundation, leave a 6mm (¼in) allowance when you trim.

4 Carefully tear away the paper foundation, if used. A muslin foundation will remain in place. Press.

⏭️▶LOG CABIN

Log cabin is a very versatile block design, usually featuring fabric strips surrounding a small central square, as shown here, though some log cabin blocks have other shapes in the centre. Blocks can be made individually or chain pieced. Always leave a 6mm (¼in) seam allowance unless otherwise stated. Log cabin is stunning in simple two-colour versions and the blocks can be set in many ways to create secondary patterns (see p.77).

METHOD 1: INDIVIDUAL BLOCKS

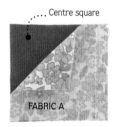
····· Centre square
FABRIC A

1 Cut a centre square of the desired size, plus seam allowances. Cut a second square the same size from fabric A and, with right sides together, stitch them together along one edge to make a pieced unit. Press open.

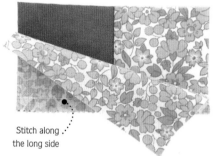
Stitch along ·· the long side

2 Cut a strip from fabric A the width of the centre square and the same length as the pressed pieced unit. With right sides together, stitch this strip to the long side of the unit.

FABRIC B

3 Add two strips from fabric B in the same way, working in a clockwise direction to ensure that the centre square remains in the middle.

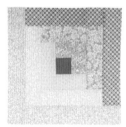

4 Continue adding strips, two from fabric A and two from fabric B, or two each from different fabrics. Always work in a clockwise direction until the block reaches the desired size.

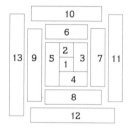

METHOD 2: COURTHOUSE STEPS VARIATION

FABRIC A
FABRIC A
FABRIC A

1 Cut a centre square. From fabric A, cut two squares the same size as the centre and with right sides together, join them to opposite sides of the centre square to make a pieced unit. Press the seams away from the centre.

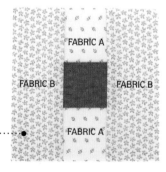
FABRIC A
FABRIC B   FABRIC B
FABRIC A

2 Cut strips the same width as the centre square from fabric B, and add one strip to each long side of the pieced unit. Trim to the same length as the pieced unit. Press away from the centre.

3 Continue adding strips – first two strips of fabric A to the top and bottom, then two of fabric B to the sides, or two each from different fabrics – until the block reaches the desired size. Press each strip away from the centre.

METHOD 3: CHAIN PIECING

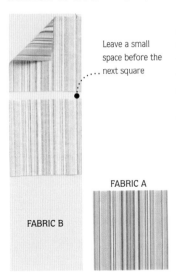

Leave a small space before the next square

FABRIC A

FABRIC B

1 Cut the required number of identical centre squares from fabric A. Cut strips from fabric B the same width as the fabric A squares. Place one centre square at one end of a strip with right sides together. Stitch, leaving a 6mm (¼in) seam allowance.

2 Without raising the machine needle or breaking the thread, leave a small gap and add a second fabric A square in the same way. Continue adding squares until you reach the end of the strip and have a chain of units.

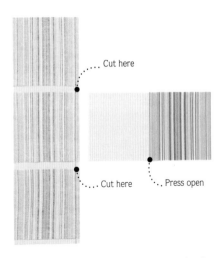

Cut here

Cut here

Press open

3 Snip the units apart and, if necessary, trim the squares so they are the same size. Flip them open and press.

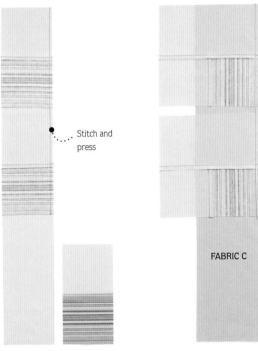

Stitch and press

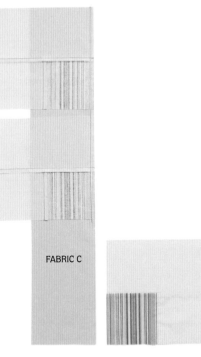

FABRIC C

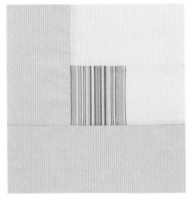

WRONG SIDE

4 Place the pieced units on a second fabric B strip, with right sides together and with the fabric A squares below the fabric B squares. Stitch and press, then cut across the strip below each fabric A square to make a number of three-part units.

5 Place the three-part units on a fabric C strip with right sides together, again with the fabric A squares at the bottom. Stitch, press, and trim, as before.

6 Repeat to add the fourth strip (fabric C) along the unstitched edge of the fabric A square, always working clockwise. Continue adding strips – two B, and then two C, or two each from different fabrics – until the blocks are the desired size.

⫸ WORKING ON A FOUNDATION

Several patchwork techniques are worked on a foundation, also known as stitch-and-flip. Crazy patchwork uses random shapes and is a great way to use up scraps. It is best made on a lightweight foundation fabric, such as calico. Reverse-pieced foundation piecing ensures accuracy and is a quick way to make blocks. You can make patterns for each segment, or cut the shapes with generous seam allowances.

FOUNDATION PIECING: TOP PIECED

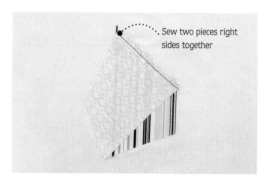
Sew two pieces right sides together

Press open the piece

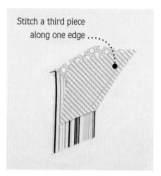
Stitch a third piece along one edge

1 Cut a foundation of lightweight calico the size you want the finished block to be plus a 2.5cm (1in) seam allowance all around.

2 Gather a selection of straight-sided pieces of various shapes and colours. Starting in the centre, place two pieces right sides together, on top of the foundation, and sew along one side through all three layers. Take a 6mm (¼in) seam allowance, whether you are working by hand or machine.

3 Press or fingerpress the pieces open.

4 Add piece 3 along one edge of the combined shape made in Step 1. Open and press. If necessary, trim the seam allowance level with scissors before you add the next piece. Snip off the thread ends.

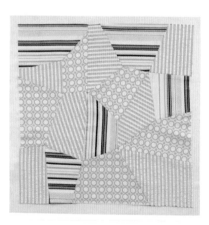

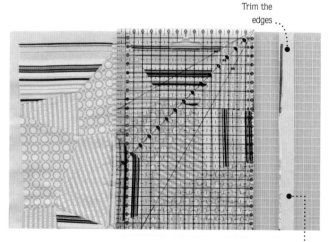
Trim the edges

5 Continue clockwise around the centre piece until the foundation is completely filled. Keep the arrangement random and avoid parallel lines. Run the seams in different directions and vary the angles. Press each piece open as you work.

6 Trim the edges level with the edges of the foundation fabric. Embellish the finished piece if you wish.

FOUNDATION PIECING: REVERSE PIECED

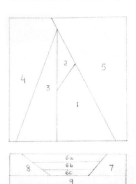

1 Cut the chosen foundation (use paper, calico, wadding, or non-woven interfacing) to size, with a generous amount added all around.

2 Trace or transfer the design to the foundation. Number the piecing order clearly on the foundation. You will be sewing from the back of the foundation, so the block will be the reverse of the foundation itself.

3 Cut out piece 1 and pin it right side up on the reverse side of the foundation. Make sure that it extends beyond the stitching lines; you can check this by holding it up to the light.

4 Cut out piece 2 and place it right sides together on piece 1, along the seam to be sewn. Pin through all layers.

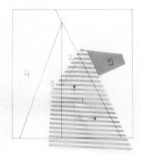

5 Turn the foundation right side up and re-pin carefully to avoid catching any pins in the feed dogs of your sewing machine.

6 Stitch the seam, joining pieces 1 and 2. If your foundation is made of paper, use a short 1.5 stitch length to make it easier to remove. If necessary, trim the seam allowance to 6mm (¼in).

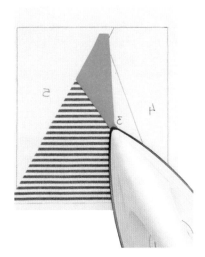

7 Turn the foundation fabric right side up, remove the pins, open the pieces, and press.

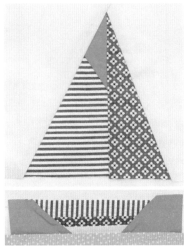

8 Cut piece 3 and align it next to piece 2. Pin it on top, then turn over and stitch as in Steps 3–7 until the top is complete. Make the bottom section in the same way.

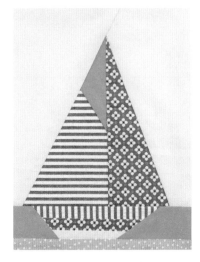

9 Join the sections. Then trim the foundation level with the edges of the patchwork design. If the foundation is removable, carefully tear it away.

➤▶ FOLDED PATCHWORK

There are a number of specialized patchwork techniques that involve manipulating fabric by folding it in specific ways before joining pieces together. They can all be used to make quilts, but because they are, by definition, made from more than one layer, they are also good for making household items, such as placemats.

CATHEDRAL WINDOW

Fold the seam allowance to the wrong side and press

1 Decide the size of the finished square (10cm/4in) and multiply the measurement by 2 (20cm/8in). Add 1.2cm (½in) seam allowance and cut four squares this size from the background, fabric A.

2 Fold the seam allowance down and press each side of the square flat. Diagonally fold one way and press, then fold along the other diagonal and press firmly to mark the exact centre. Open out.

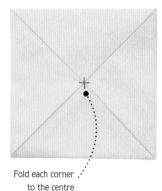

Fold each corner to the centre

3 Fold each corner of each square to the centre and press the folds firmly. Make sure that the new corners are sharply defined.

4 Take a small cross stitch across the centre into each point, through all the layers to hold the points in place.

Stitch two squares along one edge

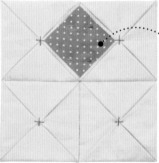

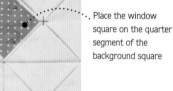

Place the window square on the quarter segment of the background square

5 Fold each corner to the centre again and press firmly. Take a small cross stitch as before through all the layers to hold the points in place. The square is now half the size of that cut in Step 1.

6 With folded edges together, join the four squares in pairs, oversewing with tiny stitches along the edge. Then join the two pairs to make a square. If you are making a large piece, you can also work in rows that are joined before the windows are added.

7 Cut four contrasting window squares from fabric B. Each window square should just fit inside a quarter segment of the background square; to work out the size, measure the distance from the centre of one folded square to the outside corner.

8 Place the first window square over a seam, on the diagonal. Pin in place. If necessary, trim the edges slightly to make it fit.

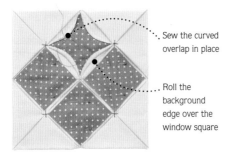

Sew the curved overlap in place

Roll the background edge over the window square

9 Roll one folded edge in the background square over the raw edge of the first window square.

10 Matching the thread to the background fabric, sew the rolled, slightly curved overlap in place with tiny stitches, catching in the raw edge completely. Do not stitch through the background fabric. Repeat to catch in the other three edges of the window.

11 Repeat Steps 7 to 9 to fill the other spaces in the square. If you work in rows, add windows after you join rows together.

SECRET GARDEN

Sew window square on points within lines

1 Make a folded square as for Steps 1 to 3 of Cathedral window (see opposite). Fold and press the corners, as in Step 4, but do not stitch in place. Cut a window square the size of the finished square.

2 Open the pressed corners and place the window square on point within the lines. If necessary, trim the raw edges to fit and anchor with small tacking stitches.

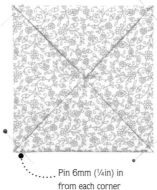

Pin 6mm (¼in) in from each corner

3 Fold the four corners of the background square into the centre. Press. Anchor each corner in the centre with a small cross, stitching through all layers.

4 Pin 6mm (¼in) in from each corner through all layers to stabilize the square.

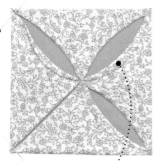

Turn over the background square edge and sew in place

5 Turn over one edge of the background square to form a curving "petal" shape. Sew in place, working outwards from the centre and using thread to match the background fabric.

6 Repeat on all eight folded edges of the background square, removing the pins and securing each corner with a double tacking stitch.

FOLDED STAR

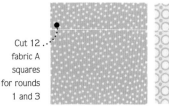

Cut 12 fabric A squares for rounds 1 and 3

Cut 16 fabric B squares for rounds 2 and 4

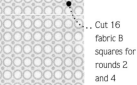

Fold the other top corner to make a right-angled triangle

Fold a top corner to the centre of the raw edges

1 The star consists of a calico foundation square with four rounds, or layers, of triangles on top. Cut the calico to the finished size plus 5cm (2in) on all sides. For rounds 1 and 3, cut 12 10cm (4in) squares from fabric A. For rounds 2 and 4, cut 16 10cm (4in) squares from fabric B.

2 For the triangles, with wrong sides together, press each square in half. Fold one top corner of the resulting rectangle to the centre of the raw edges and press. Repeat, folding the other top corner to the raw edges to make a right-angled triangle with raw edges along its long side.

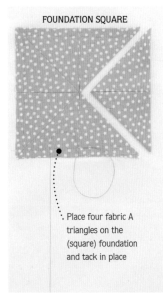

FOUNDATION SQUARE

Place four fabric A triangles on the (square) foundation and tack in place

3 To make guidelines, fold the foundation square in half horizontally and vertically and press. Fold in half again along the diagonals and press again. Open the square out.

4 For round 1, place the four fabric A right-angled triangles along the pressed guidelines, so their points meet in the centre and the folded edges are on top. Pin or tack in place along the raw edges. Secure each point with a small hidden stitch.

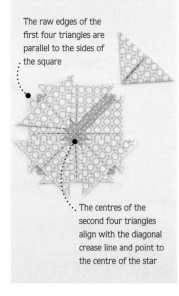

The raw edges of the first four triangles are parallel to the sides of the square

The centres of the second four triangles align with the diagonal crease line and point to the centre of the star

5 For round 2, place four fabric B right-angled triangles with their points 1cm (⅜in) from the centre, and with their raw edges parallel with the sides of the foundation square. Secure as in Step 4, then add four more fabric B triangles in the gaps, aligning their raw edges with the diagonal guidelines on the foundation square. Secure as before. Measure 1cm (⅜in) from the points and mark.

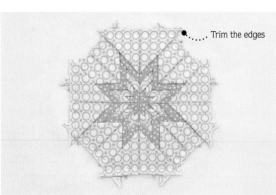

Trim the edges

6 Add eight fabric A triangles for round 3 in the same way as the eight were added for round 2, followed by eight fabric B triangles for round 4. Remove the tacking and trim and finish all the edges as desired.

⧉▶ SEMINOLE PATCHWORK

Used by the Seminole tribe of Native Americans in Florida, this type of strip-pieced patchwork is useful for borders or blocks. The method often involves cutting pieced strips at an angle and rejoining them.

METHOD 1: STRAIGHT BAND

1 Cut strips from three contrasting fabrics. Here the width of the strips from top to bottom of the picture is in the ratio of 2:1:3, plus seam allowances, which ensures that the white will be evenly offset either side of the centre line of the finished patchwork. With the narrowest strip in the centre and with right sides together, join the three strips, leaving a 6mm (¼in) seam allowance. Press the seams towards the darker colour.

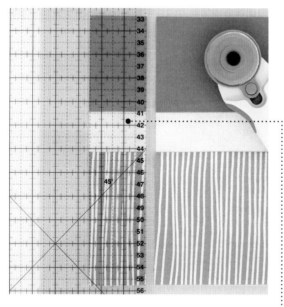

2 Using a rotary cutter and quilter's ruler, cut across the joined strips to make pieced strips of the desired width.

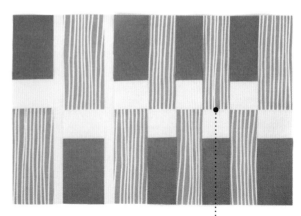

3 Alternating the top and bottom of each adjacent strip and with right sides together, sew the strips together again, leaving a 6mm (¼in) seam allowance. Press all the seams in the same direction.

METHOD 2: ANGLED BAND

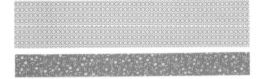

1 Cut strips from three contrasting fabrics; the widths can vary.

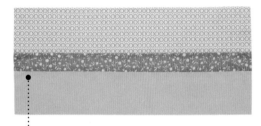

2 With right sides together and the wider strips on the outside, sew the strips together. Press the seams in the same direction.

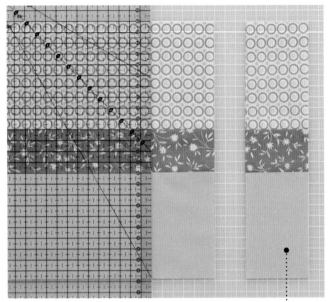

3 Using a rotary cutter and quilter's ruler, cut across the joined strips to make pieced strips of the desired width.

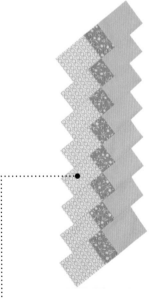

4 Sew the strips back together, leaving a 6mm (¼in) seam allowance and offsetting the centre squares each time you join one strip to the next. Press the seams in the same direction.

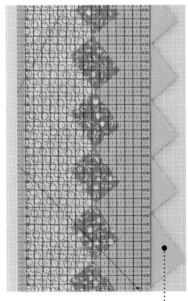

5 Using a rotary cutter and quilter's ruler, trim off the points at either edge of the pieced strip.

6 Square up both ends to make a neat pieced strip.

METHOD 3: CHEVRON BAND

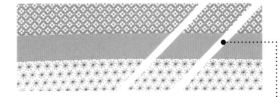

1 Cut strips the same width from three contrasting fabrics. With right sides together, sew the strips together and press the seams in the same direction. Make a second identical pieced strip.

2 Using a rotary cutter and quilter's ruler, cut one of the pieced strips several times at a 45-degree angle in one direction (see p.36) to make angled strips.

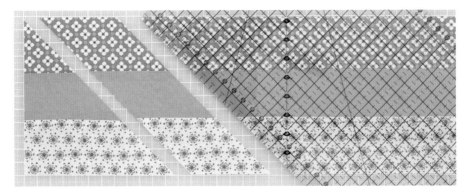

3 Repeat on the second pieced strip, using the same angle but reversing the direction of the cut.

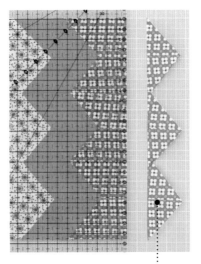

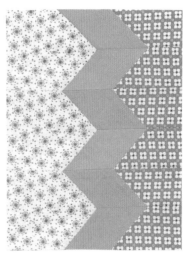

4 Match the seams of an angled strip from the first pieced strip to the seams of an angled strip from the second pieced strip. Sew together, leaving a 6mm (¼in) seam allowance. Repeat to join in pairs.

5 Join the pairs to create a chevron band. Press the seams in the same direction. Using a rotary cutter and quilter's ruler, trim off the points at either edge of the pieced strip.

6 The result is a chevron pattern running through the whole of the pieced strip.

⟫▶ FRAYED PATCHWORK

Seams do not always have to be hidden away. By sewing pieces wrong sides together the seams will show on the outside of the patchwork piece. While there are more involved ways of sewing frayed seams, the method shown below is the easiest. Do not quilt over the frayed seams as it will flatten the fluffy edges, only quilt inside the seams.

1 Piece your patchwork in the normal way, but sew all of the pieces wrong sides together. Carefully snip into the seam allowance and use a pin to tease out a few threads from the edge.

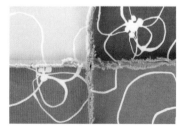

2 Putting the piece through a wash and dry cycle will really fluff up the raw edges. When the patchwork is complete it will create a lovely chenille effect, great for baby quilts.

⟫▶ YO-YOS

Yo-yos, also called Suffolk puffs, are fabric circles that have been gathered to make two layers. They are widely used as decorations in appliqué and can be further embellished. Joined edge to edge, they can be made into tablecloths, cushion covers, or openwork bedcovers. Yo-yo projects are a great way to use up small scraps of fabric.

1 Cut circles of fabric twice the desired finished size. Knot a length of strong thread, doubled if necessary, and secure it close to the edge on the wrong side of the circle. Turn the raw edge 6mm (¼in) to the wrong side and take small gathering stitches through both layers all around the edge, to make a single hem. Finish next to where you started.

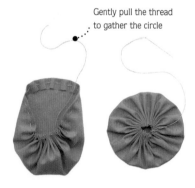

Gently pull the thread to gather the circle

2 Do not remove the needle or cut the thread, but pull the thread gently to gather the circle into a smaller one, with pleats around the centre. The raw edge will disappear inside the circle. Secure the thread with a couple of tacks or back stitches, then knot it. Cut the thread. Flatten the circle by gently fingerpressing the edges. The gathered side is usually the front, but sometimes the back is used instead.

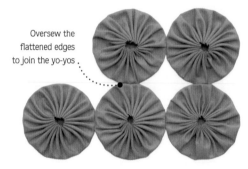

Oversew the flattened edges to join the yo-yos

3 To join yo-yos, place them gathered sides facing and oversew the flattened edges for a short distance, taking small, tight stitches. Join yo-yos together until you have a row that is the desired length; join rows together in the same way.

⋙▶ PICTORIAL BLOCKS

Most pictorial quilt blocks are appliquéd, but there are a number of representational blocks, traditional and modern, that are pieced. Many of them, such as flowers and leaves, derive from nature, and most look best if they are spaced out on a quilt, not set together edge to edge. Sashing (see pp.78–79) can be used to separate blocks to show them off, or they can be alternated with plain, solid blocks.

MAPLE LEAF: NINE-PATCH

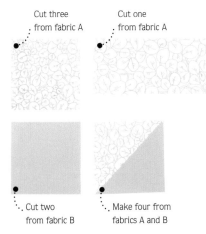

Cut three from fabric A

Cut one from fabric A

Cut two from fabric B

Make four from fabrics A and B

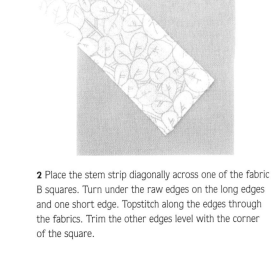

Trim the corner to level with the square

1 Divide the size of the finished block by three. Add seam allowances. Cut three squares that size from fabric A and two from fabric B. From fabric A cut a strip 4cm (1½in) wide and long enough to fit across the diagonal of one square for the "stem". Make four half-square triangles of the same size (see p.64) from fabrics A and B.

2 Place the stem strip diagonally across one of the fabric B squares. Turn under the raw edges on the long edges and one short edge. Topstitch along the edges through the fabrics. Trim the other edges level with the corner of the square.

3 Following the layout, join the units to make three rows of three blocks each.

4 Join the rows, making sure you catch the raw edge of the "stem" strip in the seams.

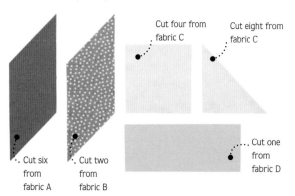

Cut four from fabric C

Cut eight from fabric C

Cut one from fabric D

Cut six from fabric A

Cut two from fabric B

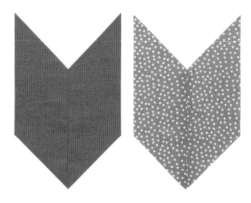

1 Cut six 45-degree angle diamonds for the "petals" from fabric A, two petals from fabric B, and four corner squares and eight right-angled triangles from fabric C (see p.37). Make sure to cut half of the petals in reverse, to form pairs. From fabric D, cut a strip 2.5cm (1in) wide and long enough to fit across the diagonal of one fabric C square for the "stem".

2 Matching the prints, join the "petals" in pairs as shown above. Apply the fabric D strip diagonally across one of the fabric C squares. Turn the raw edges under on the long edges and level both short ends even with the corners of the square (see Maple leaf, p.103). Topstitch 2mm (¹⁄₁₆in) from the folded edge to square C.

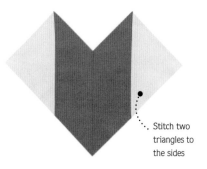

Stitch two triangles to the sides

3 Stitch a right-angled triangle to both long sides of each pair of "petals".

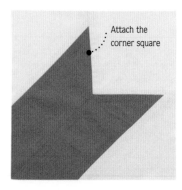

Attach the corner square

4 Set in the corner squares (see pp.74–75) to make four units. Make sure you catch the raw edges of the "stem" square in the seams.

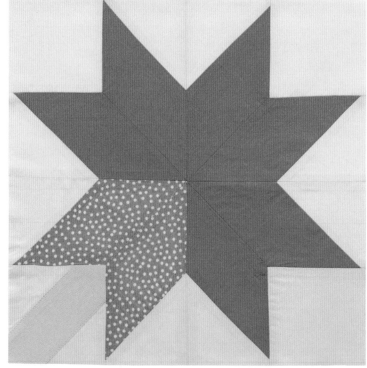

5 Stitch together the units in pairs, then stitch together the pairs, manipulating the seams in the centre to help them lie flat.

CAKE STAND BASKET: FIVE-PATCH

... Cut eight from
fabric A

... Make eight from
fabrics A and B

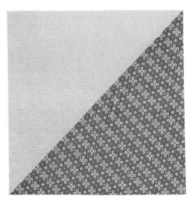

1 Divide the size of the finished block by five. Add seam allowances. Cut eight squares this size from fabric A. Make eight half-square triangles (see p.64) from fabrics A and B.

2 The finished centre half-square triangle is three times the size of the outside squares. Cut one triangle from fabric A and one from fabric B to this size and stitch them together on the diagonal.

... Stitch together
three half-square
triangles

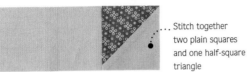

.... Stitch together
two plain squares
and one half-square
triangle

3 Stitch together three small half-square triangles, then stitch one small half-square triangle to two small plain squares. Sew the strips to opposite sides, top and bottom, of the centre half-square triangle.

4 Following the layout above, stitch the remaining small squares into two strips and sew the strips to opposite, left and right, sides of the large unit. Match all of the seams carefully.

SHIP: DOUBLE FOUR-PATCH

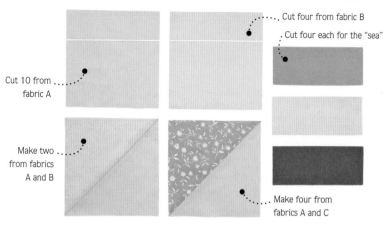

Cut 10 from fabric A

Make two from fabrics A and B

Make four from fabrics A and C

Cut four from fabric B

Cut four each for the "sea"

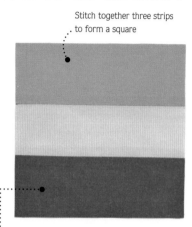

Stitch together three strips to form a square

1 The fabric requirements given here make a 30.5cm (12in) square block. Divide the size of the finished block by four (7.6cm / 3in). Add seam allowances to each side (8.8cm / 3½in). Cut 10 squares this size from fabric A, four from fabric B, and four from fabric C. Set aside four from fabric A and two from fabric B to use as squares. The others will be made into half-square triangles. Divide the finished mini block by three (7.6cm ÷ 3 [3in ÷ 3]) and add 1.2cm (½in) seam allowance to determine the size of the strips that make up the "sea" (8.8 x 3.7cm [3½ x 1½in]). Cut four strips in each of three "sea" colours to that measurement.

2 Stitch together the 8.8 x 3.7cm (3½ x 1½in) sea strips to make four units the same size as the plain squares 8.8cm (3½in). You can also make the "sea" from three long strips if you prefer. The length of each strip would be the same as the finished measurement of the block (30.5cm/12in) and the width should be the width determined in Step 1 (3.7cm/1½in).

3 Following the layout, stitch the half-square triangle units together by drawing a diagonal line from corner to corner and stitching along that line. Piece together the rows using a 6mm (¼in) seam allowance.

4 Stitch the four rows together, aligning the points to complete the block.

HOUSE

FABRIC C   FABRIC B   FABRIC A

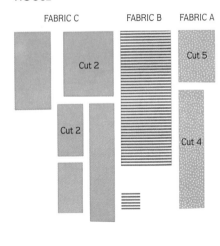

Cut 2

Cut 2

Cut 5

Cut 4

1 From fabric A, cut five 6.5 x 9cm (2½ x 3½in) rectangles and four 4 x 21.5cm (1½ x 8½in) strips. From fabric B, cut one 9 x 30.5cm (3½ x 12in) strip and one 4cm (1½in) square. From fabric C, cut two rectangles 5 x 9cm (2 x 3½in), one 8.25 x 4cm (3¼ x 1½in), and one strip 21 x 4cm (8¼ x 1½in), two rectangles 9 x 11.5cm (3½ x 4½in), and one 6.5 x 14cm (2½ x 5½in).

2 On each of the two 5 x 9cm (2 x 3½in) fabric C rectangles, draw a diagonal line from corner to corner on the wrong side of the fabric. Place a rectangle in each of the corners of the fabric B 9 x 30.5cm (3½ x 12in) rectangle, lining up the corners. Stitch through the lines and trim to a 6mm (¼in) seam allowance to create the "roof".

3 Make the chimney strip from the smallest square (fabric B) and the two narrow fabric C strips, as shown.

Make two windows

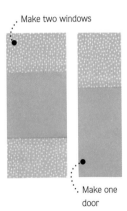

Make one door

4 Make two window units by adding a 6.5 x 9cm (2½ x 3½in) fabric A rectangle to the short ends of each 9 x 11.5cm (3½ x 4½in) fabric C rectangle.

5 Make the door unit by stitching together the remaining fabric A rectangle to the 6.5 x 14cm (2½ x 5½in) fabric C rectangle.

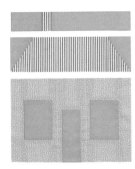

6 Stitch together the window and door units by adding the remaining four fabric A strips to the long edges. Then stitch together the chimney and roof elements.

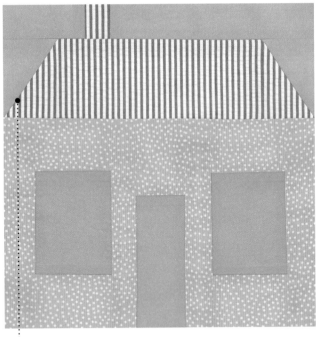

7 Stitch the roof and house together to complete the 30.5cm (12in) square block.

APPLIQUÉ

APPLIQUÉ TECHNIQUES

Appliqué is a decorative technique in which shapes are cut from one fabric and applied to a background fabric. It has been used in quiltmaking for centuries and is found on many other items, from clothing to cushions. Hand appliqué is the traditional method, but working by machine can be just as effective.

▶▶ STITCHES FOR APPLIQUÉ

Appliquéd shapes can be attached to the background in two ways, either hidden (using blind stitch) or calling attention to themselves as part of the design. Machine appliqué is almost always worked with decorative stitches such as zigzag or satin stitch, or with one of the many stitches programmed into modern sewing machines.

BLIND STITCH OR SLIP STITCH

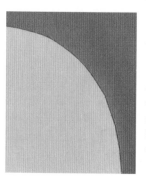

Bring the needle up on the right side of the background fabric, next to the turned-under edge of the shape being applied. Insert a few threads into the folded edge. Go back through the background fabric and continue taking tiny stitches 3mm (⅛in) apart around the entire shape.

BLANKET STITCH

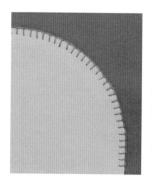

Bring the needle up on the right side of the background fabric, next to the turned-under edge of the shape being applied. Take a stitch into the shape 3–6mm (⅛–¼in) to the right and perpendicular to the edge. Bring the needle out at the edge and loop the thread under the point. Pull tight and repeat.

TIPS FOR APPLIQUÉ

• Blanket stitch (above, right) is the most popular decorative stitch for hand appliqué, but many basic embroidery stitches can be used as decoration, including cross stitch, herringbone, chain stitch, and feather stitch.

• Make sure that decorative stitches sit tight against the turned-under edge and are in proportion with the size of the applied pieces.

• In most appliqué techniques, a seam allowance has to be added to the shapes. The secret is to make an allowance that is wide enough to keep fraying at bay and narrow enough to be undetectable once it has been stitched.

• Most seam allowances for appliqué can be cut by eye, following the outline of the shape. Remember that you can trim away any excess as you work, but you can't add it once it has been removed. The ideal seam allowance is around 3mm (⅛in).

• If you need only one piece of a particular shape, draw it on tracing paper and cut it out. Pin the tracing paper shape to the fabric and cut it out, in the same way as a dressmaking pattern.

• Appliqué designs usually have a right and a wrong side. When transferring a design, make sure that the right side of the fabric will be the right way around when the shape is cut out and applied.

• Some methods call for the outline of a design to be marked on the background fabric. In this case, make sure that the outline will be covered or can be removed when the stitching is completed. Draw the design lightly on the right side of the fabric or tack around the outlines.

• When tacking, make sure that any knots are on the wrong side of the background fabric, as this will make it easier to remove the thread later.

• If the fabric is light or you have access to a lightbox, you may be able to trace from an original pattern directly onto the fabric.

• When working machine appliqué, work a practice row or two using the same fabrics as the design to make sure your settings are correct.

⏩ DEALING WITH PEAKS AND VALLEYS

Both "peaks" (shapes that come to a sharp point) and "valleys" (sharp points between two sides of a shape) can be pointed or curved, and both can be difficult to work neatly. The points of peaks should, of course, be pointed, but you risk creating a lump under the point where you turn the edges under. The seam allowance in valleys needs to be clipped to make the edge neat.

PEAKS

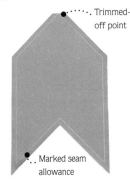

Trimmed-off point

Marked seam allowance

1 Trim the tip of the point a few threads shy of the seam allowance.

Fold the seam allowance and press

2 Fold the sides of the point along the seam allowance. Ensure that the raw edge at the point is hidden. Press the edges.

VALLEYS

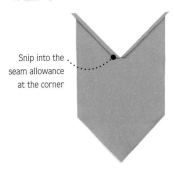

Snip into the seam allowance at the corner

At the bottom of the valley, clip to within a few threads of the marked seam allowance. Fold the edges to the wrong side. When applying the piece, take several tiny stitches in the valley to secure the cut threads.

⏩ DEALING WITH CURVES

Curves can be difficult to keep smooth. The raw edge of an outward (convex) curve is slightly longer than the folded-under edge and can cause bunching under the fold unless the seam allowance is clipped. Inward (concave) curves will sometimes stretch smoothly, but shallow curves may need to be clipped before being stitched.

CONVEX CURVES

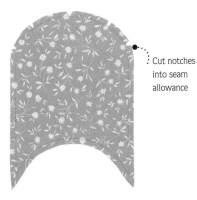

Cut notches into seam allowance

1 Cut tiny V-shaped notches into the seam allowance to remove excess fabric.

2 When it is turned under, the curved edge will lie flat.

CONCAVE CURVES

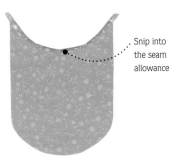

Snip into the seam allowance

Clip straight cuts into the seam allowance as you work, one section at a time. The clips will form notches that will spread open and allow the edge to lie flat.

Machine appliqué is quick and will stand many washes, especially if you use a tightly woven fabric and finish the edges with zigzag or satin stitch. Before you begin, it is a good idea to practise on scraps of the fabrics you will be using. Try out different stitch widths and lengths to see what works best.

OUTER CORNERS

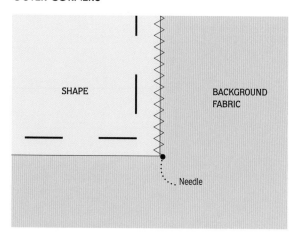

To work outer corners, stop with the needle outside the shape on the right-hand side. Lift the foot, turn the work, and continue.

INNER CORNERS

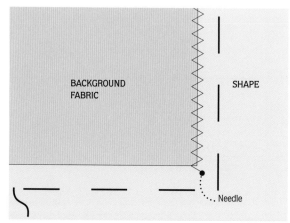

To work inner corners, stop with the needle inside the shape on the left-hand side. Lift the foot, turn the work, and continue.

CONVEX CURVES

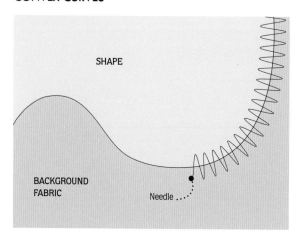

When approaching convex (outer) curves, stop with the needle just outside the shape. Lift the foot, turn the work to align it with the direction you're sewing, and continue.

CONCAVE CURVES

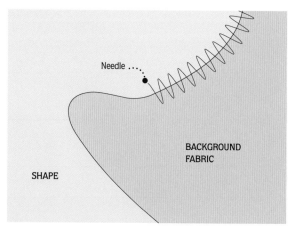

When approaching concave (inner) curves, stop with the needle inside the shape. When working any kind of curve, you may need to stop frequently to turn the work slightly, then take a few stitches, then stop, and turn again.

USING APPLIQUÉ TEMPLATES

There are many ways to make appliqué templates (see p.28), but the principle is the same for most. If you will be using the same shape over and over, it is best to use stiff card or template plastic. If you will only be using it once, use paper or tracing paper. Templates can be created for almost any shape. You can trace a pre-existing shape, or create your own hand-drawn shapes.

1 With a marker pen or pencil, draw or trace your shape onto the template material of your choice.

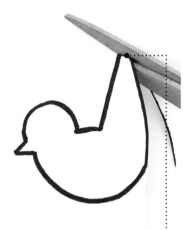

2 Using a sharp pair of scissors, not your fabric scissors, carefully cut out the shape.

3 Position the template on the fabric and trace around it with a water-soluble pen. We've used a pencil here so the lines can be easily seen.

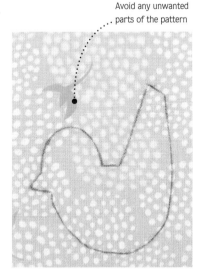

Avoid any unwanted parts of the pattern

4 Take care in positioning the template on the fabric to avoid any unwanted part of the fabric pattern on your appliqué piece.

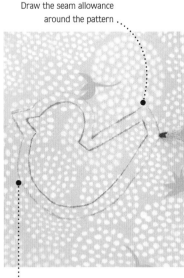

Draw the seam allowance around the pattern

5 Add a 3–6mm (⅛–¼in) seam allowance to the outside of the traced line.

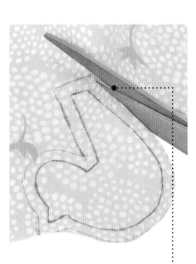

6 Using a sharp pair of fabric scissors, cut out your design along the seam allowance line.

Needle-turned or turned-edge appliqué is the traditional method for applying shapes to a background. We've used a pencil here for clarity, but you should use a water-soluble pen or other removable method to mark your fabric.

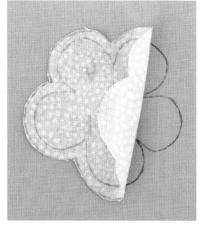

1 Make templates for the appliqué shapes. Transfer the shapes to the right side of the appliqué fabric and cut them out, adding a scant 3–6mm (⅛–¼in) seam allowance all around.

2 Wash and press the background fabric, then lay it out flat, right side up. Place the pattern on the background fabric and trace it out.

3 Place the appliqué piece in position on the background fabric and pin in place right side up.

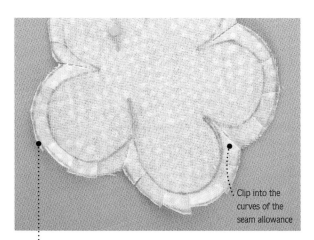

Clip into the curves of the seam allowance

Blind stitch the appliqué piece to the fabric

4 With the appliqué piece pinned in place, clip into the curves, peaks, or valleys at regular intervals along the seam allowance (see p.111).

5 With the point of the needle, turn under a small section of the seam allowance and blind stitch the appliqué piece to the background, using thread to match the appliqué fabric.

FREEZER PAPER APPLIQUÉ

Freezer paper is a stiff, white paper coated on one side with a film that can be ironed onto fabric and easily removed without leaving residue. The paper side is ideal for drawing patterns onto. It can be found in quilt shops, at some supermarkets, and online. Seam allowances can be pressed over the edge to the wrong side to give a hard crease that makes it easy to sew the shapes in place.

1 Trace the templates in reverse on the non-shiny side of the freezer paper and cut out.

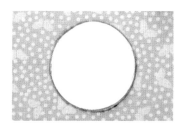

2 Place the freezer paper template on the wrong side of the appliqué fabric, shiny side down and trace around it.

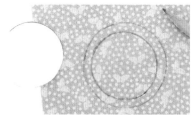

3 Add a 3–6mm (⅛–¼in) seam allowance all around, then iron the template in place. Cut around the shape on the marked seam allowance.

4 Clip or notch any peaks, valleys, or curves up to the paper (see p.111). Press the seam allowance to the wrong side, using the edge of the freezer paper as a guide. Remove the freezer paper and blind stitch the shape to the background fabric.

RAW-EDGE APPLIQUÉ

Non-woven fabrics, such as felt and felted wool, that won't fray can be used effectively in decorative appliqué, but remember that they cannot be laundered. No seam allowances are needed.

1 Trace your entire pattern onto the background fabric. Then trace the pattern pieces separately on tracing paper. Cut out each paper pattern and pin to the fabrics.

2 Cut out the appliqué pieces (without a seam allowance). Pin the first piece to the background and stitch in place, using a decorative stitch.

3 Add pieces in order. Remove all the pins and press from the wrong side.

⫸▶ HAWAIIAN APPLIQUÉ

Hawaiian appliqué originated in Hawaii when women native to the islands were taught to sew by early missionaries. The patterns are usually square and cut as eight-sided motifs from a single piece of folded fabric. The designs are traditionally based on flora indigenous to the Pacific Islands, but six-sided snowflake motifs can also be used. Finished pieces are usually echo quilted (see p.135).

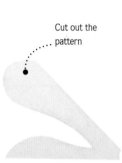

Trace the pattern on the folded paper

Cut out the pattern

1 Cut a piece of paper to the size of the finished block. Fold the paper in half twice, then along the diagonal once to make a triangle. Draw on the triangle or cut freestyle through all the layers, with the main part of the design on the folded edge.

2 Cut out one triangular section and transfer it to card to use as a template in Step 3.

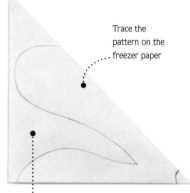

Trace the pattern on the freezer paper

3 Cut a square of freezer paper the same size as the original paper pattern. Fold it in half twice, paper side out, then fold it once along the diagonal to make a triangle. This matches the template. Transfer the template outline to the paper, making sure that the fold of the paper matches the fold on the template.

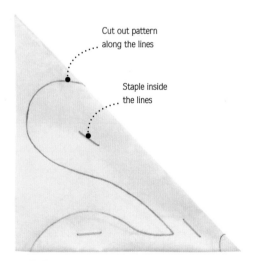

Cut out pattern along the lines

Staple inside the lines

4 Staple the layers together inside the design lines. Cut out along the marked line.

5 Remove the staples carefully and open out the paper pattern.

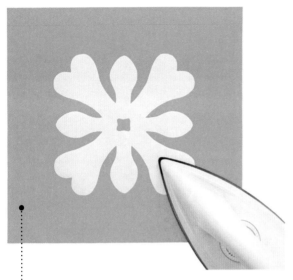

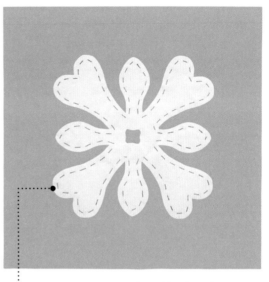

6 Cut a square of the appliqué fabric and one of the background fabric, both 5cm (2in) larger than the pattern square. Fold both in half twice to find the centre and position them, wrong side of the appliqué fabric to right side of the background fabric.

7 Centre the freezer paper pattern on the right side of the appliqué fabric, sticky side down, and iron it in position.

8 Tack the layers together 6mm (¼in) from the inside edge of the paper pattern.

Cut the fabric along the pattern and stitch

9 Work a small section at a time by cutting away the appliqué fabric along the edge of the pattern, leaving a 6mm (¼in) seam allowance. Turn the seam allowance under so that it's level with the edge of the pattern and blind stitch the fabric to the background.

10 Continue cutting and stitching until the entire pattern has been applied to the background (see p.111 for dealing with curves). Remove the tacking stitches and peel the pattern away.

⫸▶ BRODERIE PERSE

Persian embroidery, or broderie perse, is a technique in which motifs are cut from one printed fabric and applied to a different background. Several motifs, not necessarily from the same fabric, can be layered and rearranged to create a new design.

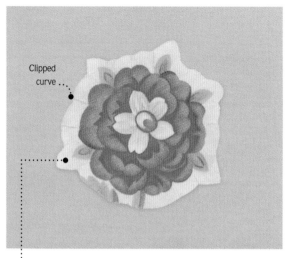

1 Cut out the motif with a generous 6mm (¼in) seam allowance. Clip any curves inside the seam allowance. If there are areas that are too small to cut away, leave the background fabric in place.

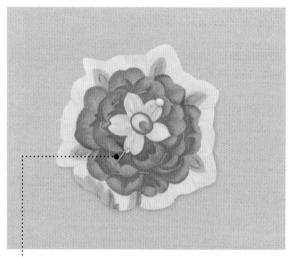

2 Pin the motif in position on the background and tack it 1.2cm (½in) inside the outline. For narrow areas such as stems, tack along the centre. Trim outside seam allowances to reduce bulk wherever possible.

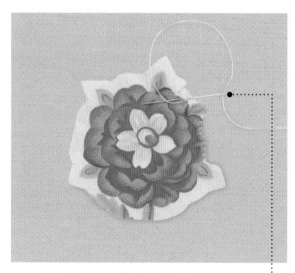

3 Using the needle tip, turn the seam allowance under and blind stitch the motif to the background, using thread to match the motif, or use a decorative stitch and contrasting thread as shown.

4 This appliqué technique allows you to make a small piece of expensive printed fabric go a long way, as individual motifs can be applied over a larger and less costly background fabric.

▶ STITCH AND CUT APPLIQUÉ

In this quick machine method, the motif is marked on the appliqué fabric and then sewn along the marked line before being cut out along the stitching line. The edges can then be finished by machine or by hand.

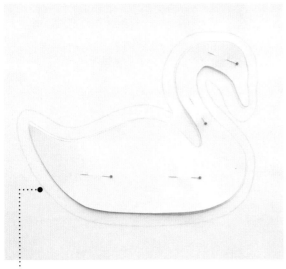

1 Make templates for the shapes. Draw around each shape on the right side of the fabric and add a 1.2cm (½in) seam allowance all around. Cut out the fabric shapes on the marked seam allowance.

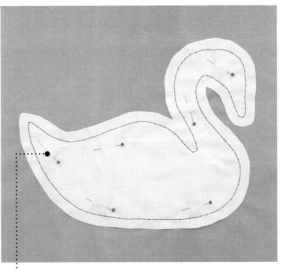

2 Pin the shapes to the background fabric, making sure that the pins will not get caught in the machine foot, and use a straight stitch to sew along the marked line.

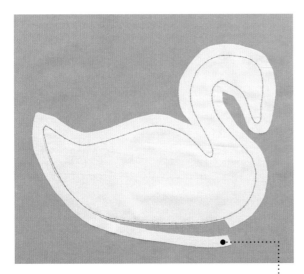

3 Using small, sharp scissors, trim away the seam allowance, cutting as close to the stitching line as possible without cutting the stitched thread.

4 Zigzag or satin stitch along the trimmed edge to finish the raw edge and hide the straight stitching.

❯❯ FUSED APPLIQUÉ

Fusible bonding web is a non-woven fabric impregnated with glue that is activated by heat. One side is anchored to paper on which shapes can be drawn. When ironed to the wrong side of a shape and then to the background fabric, it forms a firm bond that is almost impossible to remove. It is most suitable for machine appliqué because it creates a stiffness that is difficult to sew by hand.

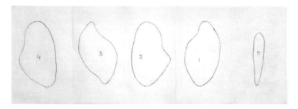

1 Transfer the shapes, in reverse, to the paper side of the web and cut them out roughly. If you group pieces that are to be cut from the same fabric close together, you can cut the whole group in one go, rather than cutting each individual shape separately.

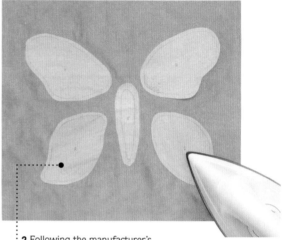

2 Following the manufacturer's instructions, place the rough, non-paper side on the wrong side of the appliqué fabric and press in place.

3 Cut out the shapes, cutting carefully along the drawn line, and peel off the backing papers. Position the shapes on the background fabric and iron in place.

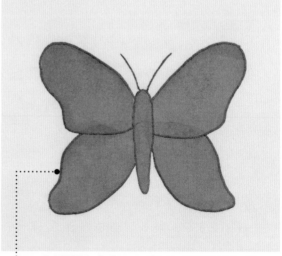

4 Finish by stitching around the edges of each appliquéd piece with machine zigzag or satin stitch.

▧▶ STAINED-GLASS APPLIQUÉ

Stained glass appliqué gets its name from the bias strips that separate the elements in the design, which resemble leading in church windows. You can make bias strips yourself (see pp.46–47) or purchase bias strips with fusible bonding web on the back, which can be ironed in place to secure the strip while you stitch it in place. If your design features straight lines, you can use strips cut on the straight grain.

1 Transfer the pattern onto the background fabric. If the design is complicated, number the shapes on the background.

2 Following the manufacturer's instructions, place the rough, non-paper side of the bonding web on the wrong side of the fabric and press in place.

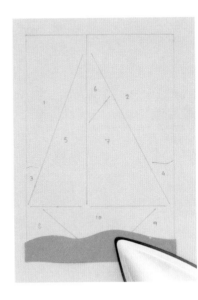

3 Cut out the appliqué shapes without adding any seam allowances. Iron them in place on the background.

4 Butt each piece up tightly against its neighbour, so that it will be easier to catch the raw edges under the bias strips.

5 Plan the order in which you apply the bias strips so that you can cover any raw ends with another strip. Iron on the strips and stitch them in place, using a machine blindstitch.

6 The bias strips cover the raw edges of the pieces over which they are placed. Continue until all of the raw edges are covered.

▤▶ REVERSE APPLIQUÉ

This technique uses two or more layers of fabric, cutting away the top layers to reveal the fabric beneath. The raw edges are turned under to finish the shape. Floral, pictorial, and geometric designs work well.

REVERSE APPLIQUÉ BY HAND

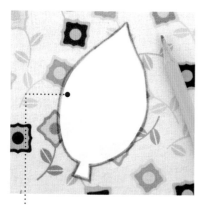

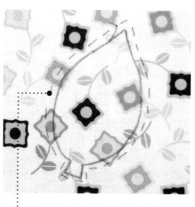

1 Choose two fabrics and pin or tack them together, right sides up, around the outside edge. Trace the motif onto a template and cut it out. Place the template right side up on top of the fabric and with a water-soluble pen, trace around the template. (We have used a pencil so that readers can see the lines easily.)

2 Remove the template and tack around the outline approximately 1cm (⅜in) from the outside edge.

3 Using small, sharp scissors, begin cutting away the shape 6mm (¼in) inside the marked line, being careful to cut only the top layer of fabric. Cut one section at a time, clipping or cutting small notches into any curves, peaks, or valleys (see p.111).

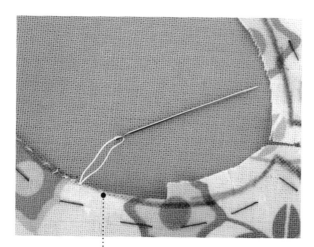

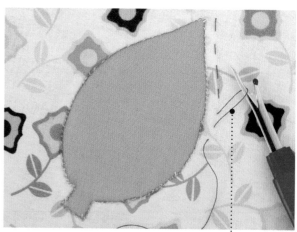

4 Turn under the seam allowance along the marked line. Using thread to match the top fabric, slip stitch the edge in place.

5 Remove all of the tacking stitches.

1 With your paper or freezer paper template in place on the top fabric, trace around the outside edge with a water-soluble pen. (We have used a pencil so that readers can see the lines easily.) Place the marked fabric on top of the bottom fabric, both right side up.

2 Using a needle and thread, tack around the traced shape approximately 1cm (⅜in) from the edge to hold both layers in place. Pin before tacking, if needed.

3 Using the traced line as a cutting guide, carefully cut through the top layer of fabric only revealing the fabric below.

4 Using your sewing machine with a tight zigzag stitch or satin stitch, encase the raw edges of the top fabric with the bottom fabric. Carefully remove the tacking stitches.

⊒▶ TURNED REVERSE APPLIQUÉ

This method uses an extra piece of fabric stitched to the main fabric and then turned through to create a window for your desired shape to show through. It is a quicker method of traditional reverse appliqué (see pp.122–123) and can give a cleaner, neater edge. This method works best on simple shapes. You may see the edges of the turned-through piece of fabric, so either use a fabric to complement your design, or the same fabric as your main fabric.

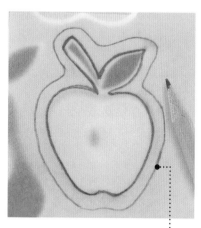

1 Choose a fabric with a motif suitable for appliqué. Using a sheet of tracing paper, trace around the object with a pencil. Add your desired space around the object.

2 Cut out the traced shape along the outside line. Place the template on the wrong side of the lining fabric to be turned through. Trace around the template.

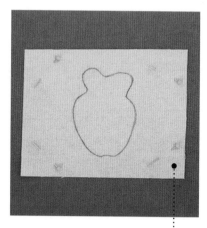

3 Position the lining fabric on the main fabric, right sides together, where you'd like the shape to appear. Pin the lining fabric in place.

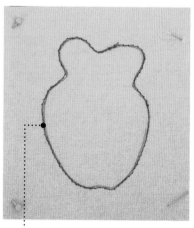

4 Using a sewing machine, stitch along the motif outline through both the layers of fabric.

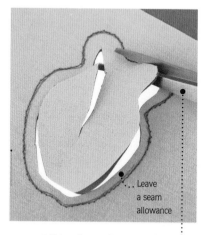

Leave a seam allowance

5 Using sharp scissors, cut inside of the stitched shape leaving approximately a 3–6mm (⅛–¼in) seam allowance.

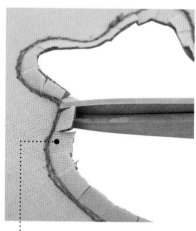

6 Snip into any curves and trim any points without cutting through the stitching.

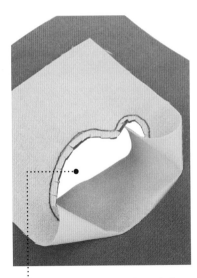

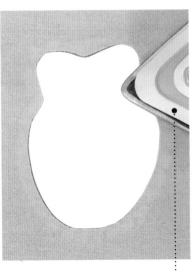

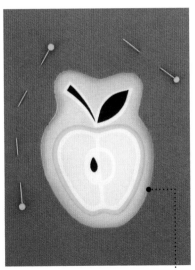

7 Push the lining fabric through the hole to the wrong side of the main fabric and out the other side.

8 Press the edges flat on the lining side to get a neat finished look.

9 With the main fabric facing up, position the fabric with the motif underneath, making sure that the motif is centred inside the cut-out shape. Pin in place.

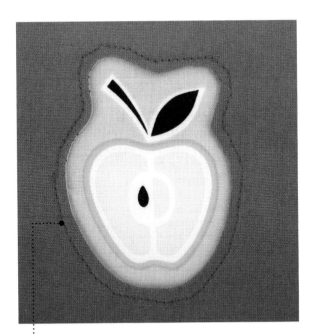

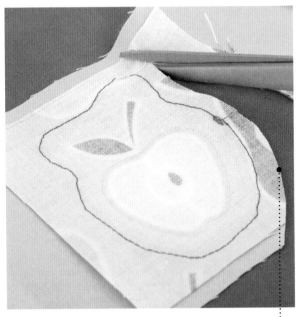

10 Using a matching or complementary thread, topstitch about 3mm (⅛in) from the edge to secure all the layers together.

11 Trim off the excess fabric from around the stitched shape on the back side of the piece. Be careful not to cut the main fabric or the stitches.

The edges of appliquéd pieces need not always be neatly finished. Leaving the edges frayed gives a casual and worn look to an appliqué piece. This technique works well on items for kids. You can add interfacing to the back of the appliqué piece, just inside the seam allowance, to give it more stability and to keep the edges from fraying back too far and the shape from becoming detached.

Trim the fabric to your desired shape

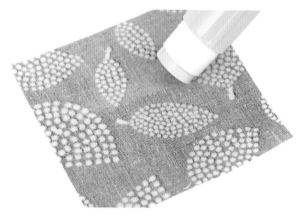

1 Cut out the shape you wish to attach to your main fabric adding a 1cm (⅜in) seam allowance all around. If you'd like to interface the shape to give it more stability, cut a piece of interfacing the same size as the shape, without the seam allowance and apply it to the wrong side of the shape.

2 Using a fabric glue stick designed for appliqué, lightly apply glue to the wrong side of the shape. If you are not using a fabric glue stick, skip to Step 3.

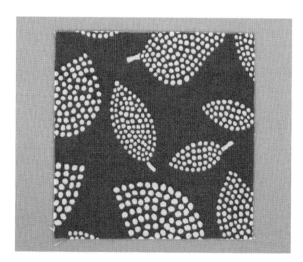

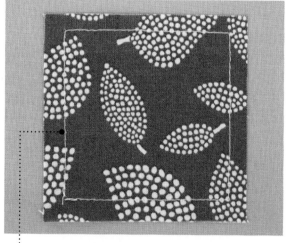

3 Position the shape in place on the right side of the background fabric. If you used glue, go to Step 4. If not, pin or tack the shape in place.

4 Using your sewing machine or a needle and thread, stitch through both layers inside the edge of the appliqué shape leaving a 1cm (⅜in) seam allowance. Remove any pins or tacking stitches. The edges will fray over time, but to speed up the process you can put the finished item through a normal wash and dry cycle, to roughen up the free edges.

⫸▶ FREE-MOTION APPLIQUÉ

Free-motion appliqué uses the same idea as frayed-edge appliqué, but the shapes are stitched on using a free-motion, or darning, foot. Stitch around each shape as many times as you wish. Often, the piece looks best when you've stitched around it a few times, slightly altering the stitching line with each pass. See page 137 for troubleshooting information on sewing with a free-motion foot.

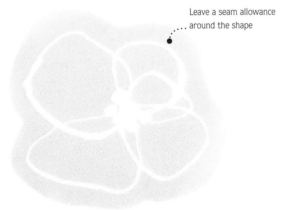

Leave a seam allowance around the shape

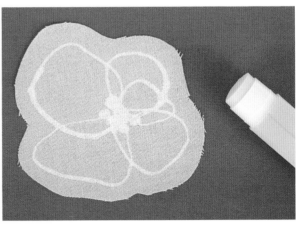

1 With a sharp pair of fabric scissors, cut out the desired shape from your fabric of choice leaving approximately a 1cm (⅜in) seam allowance.

2 Using a fabric glue stick, pins, or tacking stitches, position the shape in place on the right side of the background fabric.

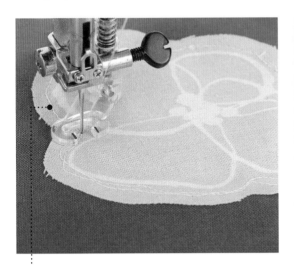

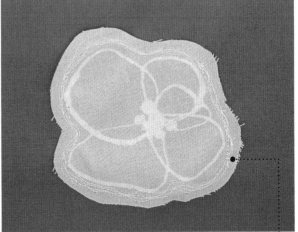

3 Using your sewing machine and a free-motion sewing foot, stitch inside the edge of the appliqué fabric. The free-motion foot will allow you to easily stitch the free-form shape of your choice.

4 Stitch around the shape as many times as you desire, then remove the pins or tacking stitches, if used. Over time, the edges will fray, but you can speed up this process by putting the finished item through a normal wash and dry cycle.

QUILTING

QUILTING TECHNIQUES

Quilting holds the layers of a quilt together, gives a quilt its texture, and should add to the overall beauty of the piece. Quilting motifs range from geometric grids and simple heart shapes to elaborate scrolls. Some appliqué motifs look best if they are outlined or echoed by quilting.

▶▶ TRANSFERRING DESIGNS

Once the quilt top is finished, you need to transfer the quilting pattern onto it. Use equipment that can be easily removed, such as water- or air-soluble pens or light pencil marks, to mark the pattern. Tailor's chalk applied lightly can usually be removed. Slivers of soap can make effective and washable marks on dark fabrics. Dressmaker's carbon paper is indelible and not recommended.

MASKING TAPE

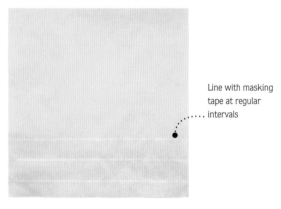

Line with masking tape at regular intervals

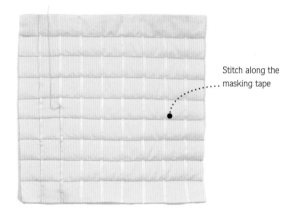

Stitch along the masking tape

1 This method only works for quilting designs in straight lines. After the quilt has been layered with wadding and backing, apply 6mm (¼in) masking tape in lines as a guide.

2 Stitch along the edge of the tape by hand or machine, then remove the tape as soon as possible. When the rows are complete, repeat in the other direction.

TRACING

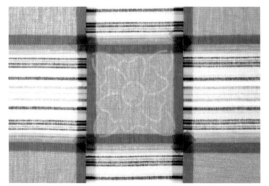

If your project is small and light in colour, you can trace the pattern directly on the fabric. Place the quilt top over the pattern on a lightbox or a glass-top table with a table lamp underneath. Alternatively, tape it to a clean window. Trace the design lightly onto the fabric.

TEMPLATES OR STENCILS

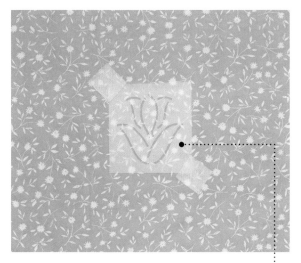

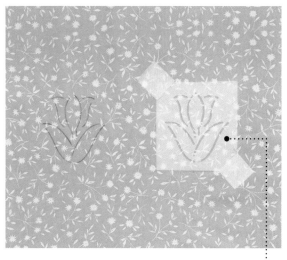

1 Mark the design on the finished quilt top before making the quilt sandwich. Place the pattern on the quilt top and secure it with masking tape or weights. Draw around a template or in the channels of a stencil with a very sharp pencil. Keep the line as light as possible.

2 Move the pattern as necessary and repeat until the entire top has been marked.

TRACE AND TACK

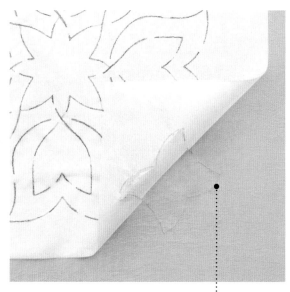

1 Use on fabrics that are hard to mark. Transfer the pattern to the quilt top before making the quilt sandwich. Transfer the design to tissue paper and pin in place. With the knot on top, sew along the pattern lines with a small running stitch. Secure with a double backstitch.

2 Pull the paper away gently without disturbing the tacking. If necessary, score the marked lines with a pin to break the paper.

⫸ HAND QUILTING BASICS

Quilting by hand gives a soft look. Straight, even stitches are worked, ideally with the needle at an angle of 90 degrees, and the same stitch length on front and back. Because of the thickness of the quilt layers, the stitches are executed using a technique known as "rocking" the needle, which uses both hands. Use quilting threads and needles, and wear a thimble on your middle finger and a protective guard underneath.

KNOTTING TO BEGIN

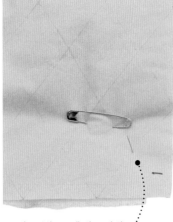

1 Knot a 50cm (20in) length of quilting thread. Take the needle down through the top layer of fabric, about 2.5cm (1in) away from where you wish to start stitching. Bring it out where you wish to begin.

Insert the needle through the fabric and pull it out where you wish to begin

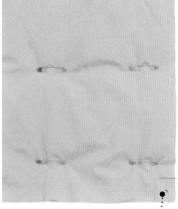

2 Pull the thread gently until the knot pops through the top layer of fabric but not hard enough to bring it out again. The knot will bury itself in the wadding and be virtually undetectable.

Pull the knot gently through the fabric

FINISHING OFF

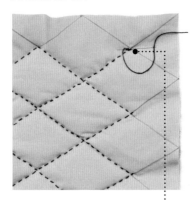

1 To secure the thread at the end, take a small backstitch through the top layer and pull the thread through to the top. Make a French knot close to the end of the stitching. Secure the wraps with your finger and pull the knot tight.

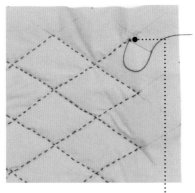

2 Insert the needle point into the top layer only, next to where the thread emerges and in the opposite direction to the stitching. Slide the needle within the wadding and bring it out about 2cm (¾in) from the end of the stitching. Gently pull the French knot through into the wadding.

3 Carefully cut the thread close to the surface and let the tail sink into the wadding.

QUILTING OR ROCKING STITCH

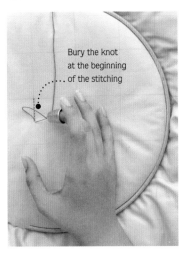

Bury the knot at the beginning of the stitching

1 Place the area to be worked inside a large embroidery hoop. Bury the knot as in Knotting to begin (see opposite). Place one hand under the quilt where the needle should emerge.

2 With the needle between thumb and forefinger of your needle hand, push the needle with your thimbled finger straight down until you feel the point with your underneath hand. Stop pushing.

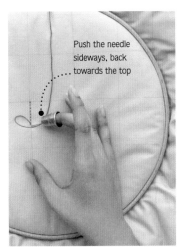

Push the needle sideways, back towards the top

3 With your underneath finger, push up gently against the side of the needle and the quilt. At the same time, push down with your top thumb and make a bump in the layers while you push the needle sideways back through to the top. Stop pushing when the length of the needle protruding on the top is the same length as the next stitch.

Push with your thumb to bring the needle through

4 Use the thimbled finger to bring the eye of the needle upright again, while at the same time pushing in front of it with your thumb. When the needle is upright and the point breaks through the fabric, push down as in Step 1.

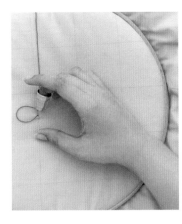

5 Continue this motion until the needle has as many stitches as it will hold. Pull the needle and thread through. Repeat.

STAB STITCH

1 Place the area to be worked inside a large embroidery hoop. Stab stitch is an alternative way to work on thick quilts. Use a thimble on each middle finger. Bury the knot as in Knotting to begin (see opposite). Push the upright needle straight down through all layers. Pull the needle and thread through to the back.

2 Push the upright needle back up through all layers, working a stitch length away from the previous stitch. Pull the needle and thread through to the top. Repeat.

▓▶ MACHINE QUILTING BASICS

Beautifully machined quilts are in no way second best to those worked by hand. Because the stitches are continuous, the finished product is usually flatter than a hand-quilted one. An even-feed, or "walking", foot, which feeds the layers through at the same speed top and bottom, is useful. Start and finish either by setting the stitch length to 0 and taking a few stitches before resetting, or leave a tail of thread to tie off.

PREPARING A QUILT FOR MACHINING

1 To work on a small area at a time, roll up both sides of the quilt towards the centre, leaving 30cm (12in) open in between. Hold the edges with clips.

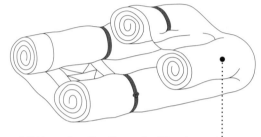

2 Fold or roll up the other ends of the piece and secure them using clips, leaving space to work on. Repeat the rolling and/or folding process as you work your way around the piece.

▓▶ GRID PATTERNS

Traditional gridded quilting patterns can be square or diamond shaped. Mark the grid by drawing the centre line in each direction, or use 6mm (¼in) masking tape.

If you set a quilting guide on your walking foot, you can use it to measure the distance between rows as you work.

1 Take a few short stitches. Set the quilting guide to the correct distance on one side and stitch the first marked row from edge to edge. Turn the work and use the quilting guide to measure each vertical row in turn.

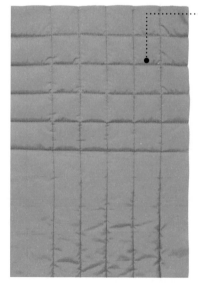

2 Repeat to work the horizontal rows.

⏩ CONCENTRIC QUILTING

Concentric quilting lines can be worked by hand or machine. Outline quilting emphasizes a pieced or appliquéd design and requires minimal marking. Straight lines can be marked with 6mm (¼in) masking tape; curves can be drawn lightly. Echo quilting is similar, but consists of a series of evenly spaced concentric quilted lines. It is most often used in Hawaiian appliqué (see pp.116–117).

OUTLINE QUILTING

Following the seamlines or outlines of the motif, work your quilting stitches 6mm (¼in) inside or outside, or on both sides, of the motif's edges.

ECHO QUILTING

Make a row of outline quilting (see left). Then continue to add evenly spaced rows to fill the background around the motif.

⏩ SEEDING

This hand-quilting method uses small, straight stitches to fill the background. The back of the piece will have longer, stranded stitches, so this is best used on pieces where the back will not show, such as wall hangings or items with linings.

1 Bury the knot (see p.132). Bring the needle and thread out near the motif. Take to the back and come up a short distance away from the first stitch.

2 Take another stitch straight down and pull the thread through and come up a short distance away. Work outwards from the motif. Keep the stitches small on the front and position them randomly so that they look like scattered seeds.

⏩ QUILTING IN THE DITCH

Here, the stitching follows the piecing lines on the quilt top and is hidden in the seams. It is best to use a walking foot on your machine when quilting in the ditch. Stitch along each row of piecing in turn, working from the centre outwards. Stop and start as little as possible.

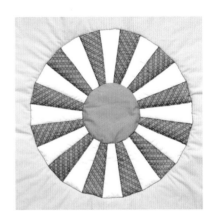

▶ CORDED QUILTING AND TRAPUNTO

Corded quilting, or Italian quilting, and trapunto, or stuffed quilting, are techniques that can be used separately, but they work well together. Both involve stitching a design through a top and a thin backing layer, usually of butter muslin. The motif is then filled from the back with lengths of quilting, knitting wool or soft cord, or with stuffing material. The outline is traditionally worked by hand.

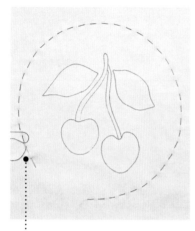

1 Cut a background fabric and transfer the design to the right side, using a water-soluble pen. Cut a piece of butter muslin or similar fabric the same size. Tack them together around the edges.

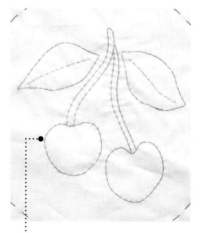

2 Outline the motif(s) with a small running stitch. Here we have used a contrasting colour thread for clarity. Where lines meet, keep stitches separate so they don't cross over. When stitching is complete, remove the marking.

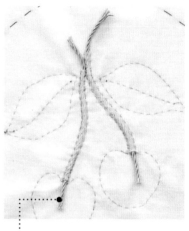

3 Thread a tapestry needle with quilting or knitting wool or soft cord. From the back, slip the needle through the first channel, leaving a short tail at each end.

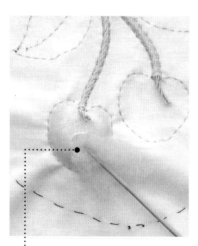

4 Make small slits in the centre of each element through the backing layer only and stuff small pieces of wadding between the top and the muslin.

5 Close each slit in the backing with a crossed stitch, such as herringbone. Remove the tacking stitches once the design is complete.

6 The cording and trapunto gives the finished motif a three-dimensional quality on the right side.

⏩ TYING

This involves tying lengths of cotton thread, lightweight wool, or ribbon through the layers of a quilt to hold them together. Use a sharp-pointed needle with an eye that is large enough to hold the thread but small enough to avoid making holes in the quilt. Space the ties according to the type of wadding, the block pattern, and the size of the quilt. Cotton and wool wadding shift easily and should be tied more closely than polyester. A general guide is 10–15cm (4–6in) apart.

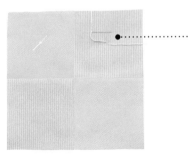

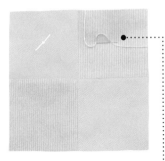

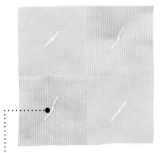

1 Working from the centre out, take a stitch down and back up through all the layers and pull the needle and thread through, leaving a 10cm (4in) tail on the top.

2 Take a second stitch in the same way in the same place.

3 Tie the ends of thread in a reef knot. Cut the thread from the reel and trim the ends to the same length. Repeat, double-stitching and knotting over the entire quilt.

⏩ FREESTYLE OR FREE-MOTION QUILTING

Freestyle, or free-motion, quilting gives machine quilters freedom to create their own designs. Mastering the technique requires patience and practice, but the effort can be very rewarding. You need a darning foot or a free-motion foot and to know how to lower the feed dogs. If your machine has the option to stop work with the needle always down, use it.

1 With the presser foot down where you will start, take one stitch. Hold the top thread and use it to gently pull the bobbin thread to the top. Secure with a few very short stitches. Start slowly and take a few more short stitches. Cut away the thread tails.

2 Guide the fabric with your hands, moving the work in any direction. Position your hands in an open circle around the machine foot and press the layers gently. Keep a moderate speed and make the stitches the same length. Tie off with a few short stitches, as in Step 1.

TROUBLESHOOTING

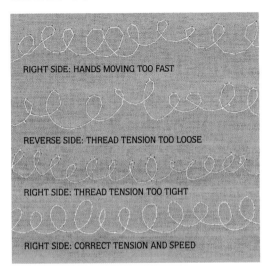

RIGHT SIDE: HANDS MOVING TOO FAST

REVERSE SIDE: THREAD TENSION TOO LOOSE

RIGHT SIDE: THREAD TENSION TOO TIGHT

RIGHT SIDE: CORRECT TENSION AND SPEED

⧓▶ EMBELLISHING QUILTS

From surface embroidery and beading to adding buttons, bows, and found objects, the ways to embellish a quilt are endless. You can use sequins, charms, or shisha mirrors, or add machine embroidery.

BUTTONS

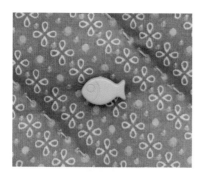

Novelty buttons make charming embellishments on theme quilts or folk-art versions. Buttons can also become "flowers" at the end of stems in a basket or accents in any number of places. Stitch buttons to the quilt top and knot them if you don't want to stitch through the backing. Otherwise, tie a knot at the back. They are best reserved for decorative pieces such as wall hangings and should not be used on quilts for children and babies, since they can become detached.

CHARMS

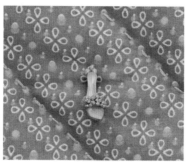

Simply tie charms in position on the quilt top, depending on the type and size. Charms are usually used to add a personal touch to a quilt – wedding motifs for a bride's quilt, for example. They are best reserved for decorative pieces such as wall hangings and should not be used on quilts for children and babies, since they can become detached.

BOWS

Tie ribbon bows to the desired size and stitch them in place on the quilt top. They can be single or double bows. Make sure the knot is secure before stitching. If adding bows to a baby quilt be sure the tail ends are not long enough to present a hazard. You can stitch a few small stitches through the central knot in the bow to help prevent it from unknotting.

⧓▶ CORDING AND PIPING

Quilted cushion covers, home accessories, or bags often require a contrasting decorative edging of cording or piping. Cording is the easiest to apply; however, with piping your choice of colour is unlimited.

SEWING ON CORDING

Tack the cording in place

1 Sew cording in between two layers of fabric, for example, along the seamline of a cushion cover. Align the fabric edge of the cording with the raw edge of the right side of the front piece. Tack in place along the edges.

2 Lay the back piece over the cording, with the right sides of the fabric pieces together, and machine stitch along the outer edge of the cording using a zip foot.

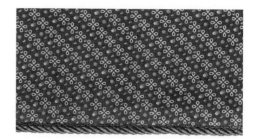

3 Remove the tacking and turn the fabric pieces right-side out. Press the fabric away from the cord so that the cord sits neatly along the seamline.

COVERING AND INSERTING PIPING CORD

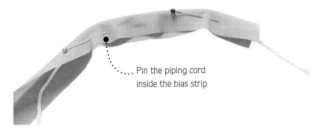

Pin the piping cord
inside the bias strip

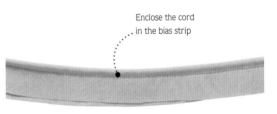

Enclose the cord
in the bias strip

1 Prepare bias strips approximately 4cm (1½in) wide (see pp.46–47). Fold the bias cut fabric strip in half, wrong side to wrong side, over the piping cord. Pin or tack in place.

2 Machine stitch in place close to the cord using a zip foot or special piping foot. If the zip foot doesn't run smoothly against the covered cord, tack the fabric in place before machine stitching.

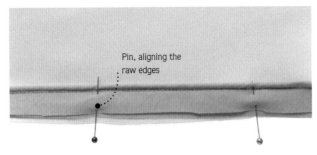

Pin, aligning the
raw edges

3 Trim the seam allowance on the piping cover so that it is the desired seam allowance width – it can be less than this width, but not more. Align the seam on the piping cover with the intended seamline on the right side of the front of the fabric and pin. Tack in place with the piping facing inwards.

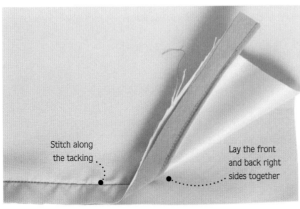

Stitch along
the tacking

Lay the front
and back right
sides together

4 If you are sewing the piping around a corner, bend it carefully to form a 90-degree angle and continue tacking.

5 Place the back fabric piece over the front piece with the right sides together and pin. Using a zip foot, machine stitch the layers together, stitching on top of the piping cord seam.

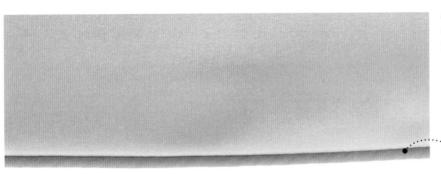

6 Turn the piece right-side out and carefully press the fabric away from the piping.

The piping sits in the
seam between the
front and back

▓▶ FASTENINGS

Although fastenings have a practical use – securing closings on cushion covers, bags, garments, and home accessories – many of them also serve as decorative finishing details. Techniques for adding very simple fastenings are provided here, including hand-stitched buttonholes, press studs, and zips.

SEWING ON BUTTONS

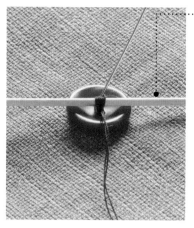

1 Thread your needle with a double strand of thread. Secure the thread to the fabric where the button is to be positioned. Pass the needle up through one hole of the button, down through the other hole to the back. Do not pull the thread taut yet – first insert a cocktail stick (or match stick) under the stitch. Then pull the thread taut. Continue working back and forth through the holes of the button and the fabric, until at least five stitches have been worked.

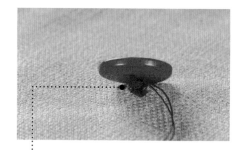

2 Remove the cocktail stick. Wrap the working thread several times around the thread under the button to form a shank. Secure the thread end with three small stitches at the back.

HAND-STITCHED BUTTONHOLES

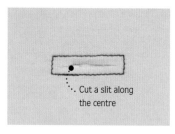

Cut a slit along the centre

1 Mark the desired finished length of the buttonhole on the right side of the piece, then machine stitch a rectangle 6mm (¼in) wide and as long as the required finished buttonhole length. Carefully cut a slit along the exact centre of this rectangle.

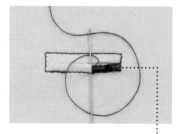

2 Using a thick, strong buttonhole thread, work tailor's buttonhole stitch (as shown) along both edges of the slit. Insert the needle through the fabric just outside the machine stitches, so that the stitches are 3mm (⅛in) long.

3 Finish each end of the buttonhole with three or four stitches that are the same width as the total width of the buttonhole. Always work buttonholes through two layers of fabric that have an interfacing in between them.

SEWING ON PRESS STUDS

Secure the press studs with several stitches......

Although press studs, or poppers, are not visible, align them carefully when sewing them on. Use a doubled thread and work three or more stitches through each hole around the edge of the press stud pieces.

SEWING ON A ZIP

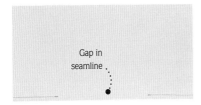

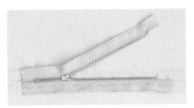

1 The easiest method for sewing on a zip is centring it on an opening in a seamline. To begin, machine stitch the seamline, leaving a gap in the stitches that is the length of the zip.

2 Tack the opening closed, working the tacking stitches along the seamline.

3 Open out the seam and press the seam allowance open on the wrong side. Open the zip and place it face down on top of the wrong side of the seam. Centring the zip teeth carefully on top of the seam, tack one side of the zip tape in place 3mm (⅛in) from the teeth.

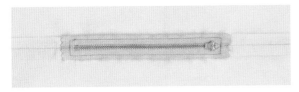

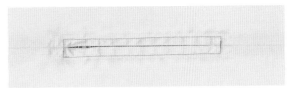

4 Close the zip and tack the other side of the zip tape in place. Using a matching thread, machine stitch the zip in place, stitching on the right side of the fabric and forming a rectangle around the zip just outside the tacking stitches.

5 Remove the tacking around the zip tape and along the opening. Press.

▶▶INSERTING TRIM IN A SEAM

If a piece is backed, trims, in addition to piping (see p.139), can be inserted between the top and the other layer, such as in the seam joining the front and back of a cushion or place mat.

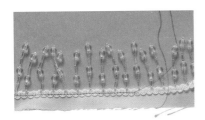

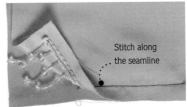

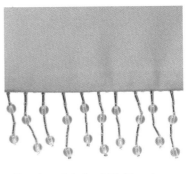

1 Measure the edge to be trimmed and add an extra 10–15cm (4–6in) to the trimming. Starting in the centre of the bottom edge on the right side of the top, align the top edge of the trim on the seamline with the decorative edge pointing away from the raw edge. Pin and tack, then machine stitch in place.

2 With the trim inside and pointing inwards, position the back and top right sides facing. Machine stitch along the same seamline that was made in Step 1.

3 Turn through to the right side and press on both sides. Topstitch along the edge if desired.

PROJECTS

PATCHWORK STRIP CUSHION

This super simple, visually appealing cushion can be made in less than an hour. Depending on the fabrics you choose, the design possibilities are endless and can produce any number of different effects. Try fussy cutting some of the patches.

DIFFICULTY LEVEL
Easy

SIZE
40 x 40cm (16 x 16in)

TOOLS AND MATERIALS
Rotary cutter
Cutting mat
Quilter's ruler
Sewing machine
Threads to match your fabrics
Pins
Iron and ironing board
Scissors
Cushion pad 40 x 40cm (16 x 16in)

FABRICS
Nine scraps of coordinating fabric to
    make nine squares, 6.5 x 6.5cm
    (2½ x 2½in) each
90 x 42cm (36 x 16½in) main fabric

SKILLS
Joining two or more strips (see p.60)

SEAM ALLOWANCE
6mm (¼in) throughout, unless
    otherwise stated

▶▶ PATTERN

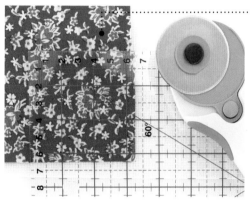

1 Cut nine scraps of coordinating fabric, each 6.5cm (2½in) square. Use the rotary cutter, mat, and quilter's ruler to make sure that each piece is perfectly square. If there is a particular part of a fabric that you'd like to appear in the centre of a square, centre it as you cut (see p.38, Fussy cutting).

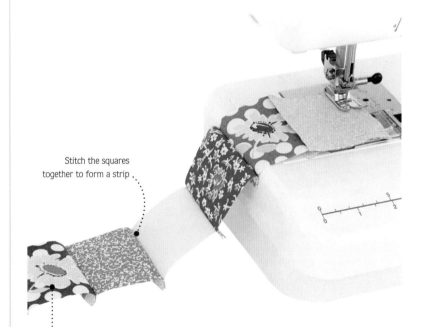

Stitch the squares together to form a strip

2 Join the nine fabric squares into a patchwork strip (see p.60) in the order you'd like to see them. Place each square in turn right sides together with the next square, pin along the edges to be joined, and sew them together. Secure each seam at the end with a few backstitches.

3 Lay the strip face down and press the seams flat to one side.

Press the seam towards the main fabric

4 Cut the two panels for the cushion front from the main fabric, one 24 x 42cm (9½ x 16½in) and another 14 x 42cm (5½ x 16½in). With right sides together, pin the long edge of the patchwork strip to one of the long edges of a front panel. Sew along the edge.

5 Open up the two pieces and on the wrong side of the fabric, press the seam towards the main fabric. With right sides together, pin the other long edge of the patchwork strip to one of the long edges of the other front panel. Sew along the edge.

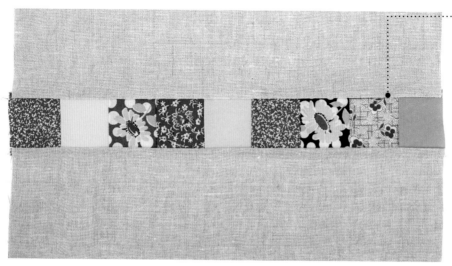

6 Open up the two pieces and on the wrong side press the seam towards the main fabric. You have now completed the cushion front.

Fold the hem twice
and pin in place

WRONG SIDE OF FABRIC

7 To make the cushion back, cut two pieces from the main fabric, each 42 x 26cm (16½ x 10in). Fold one of the long edges of one piece to the wrong side of the fabric by 1cm (⅜in). Fold it again by the same amount to create a neat hem. To enclose the raw edge, pin the hem in place, checking that it is straight, then sew along the edge of the second fold to secure the hem. Repeat on the other piece of fabric.

8 Lay the cushion front, right side up. Place one of the back pieces on top, right side down, aligning its long, unhemmed edge with the top raw edge of the cushion front. Place the second back piece right side down on top of the first, aligning its long, unhemmed edge with the bottom raw edge of the cushion front. The two back pieces should overlap. Pin along all four edges.

Machine stitch around
the edges, removing
the pins as you go

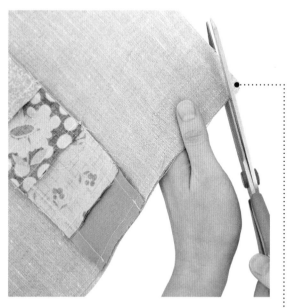

9 Leaving a 6mm (¼in) seam allowance, sew around all four edges of the cushion cover to secure the back pieces to the cushion front. Forward and backstitch over the hemmed, overlapping edges of the flaps to secure them in place. Remove the pins as you work.

10 Snip off all four corners, taking care not to cut through the stitches. Turn the cushion cover to the right side through the opening in the back. Iron, then insert the cushion pad.

BRICK QUILT

Piecing simple strips together is a great way for a beginner to get into patchwork. You get fast results without having to master any complicated techniques. This colourful single quilt is set off beautifully by its contrast backing and binding.

DIFFICULTY LEVEL
Easy

SIZE
125 x 145cm (49 x 57in)

TOOLS AND MATERIALS
Measuring tape
Quilter's ruler
Rotary cutter
Cutting mat
Pins
Sewing machine
Threads to match your fabrics
Scissors
Iron and ironing board
Safety pins
Sewing needle

FABRICS
1 fabric Jelly Roll™
560cm (220in) pre-made bias binding
    or 46 x 112cm (18 x 44in) fabric for
    double-fold binding
356 x 112cm (140 x 44in) backing fabric
    140 x 160cm (55 x 64in) wadding

SKILLS
Piecing strips (see p.60)
Chain piecing (see p.61)
Making a bigger backing (see p.45)
Binding (see pp.48–51)
Quilting in the ditch (see p.135)

SEAM ALLOWANCE
6mm (¼in) throughout, unless
    otherwise stated

TIP
The layout of the quilt is random so just
    arrange the strips in a pleasing order.

⬛▶ PATTERN

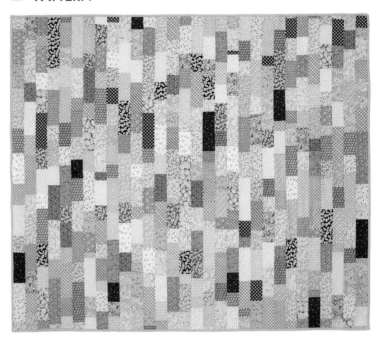

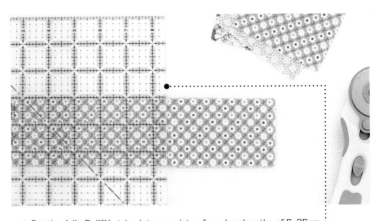

1 Cut the Jelly Roll™ strips into a variety of random lengths of 5–25cm (2–10in), with most pieces about 12cm (5in) long. Use the quilter's ruler to make sure you cut them with straight, square edges. You can lay several strips on top of each other and cut them all at the same time.

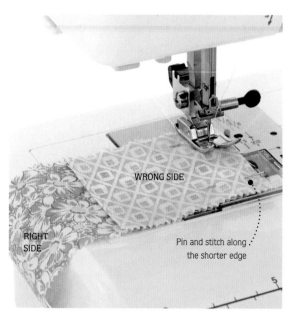

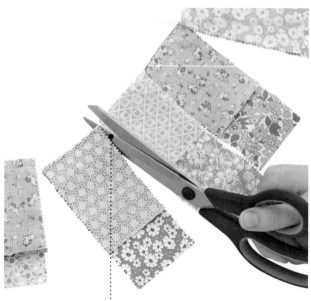

2 With right sides together, pair each fabric strip with a strip of a different length and pattern. Align the short edges and pin together. When each piece has been paired, chain piece them together (see p.61).

3 Using scissors, cut the paired pieces apart by snipping through the short length of thread between them.

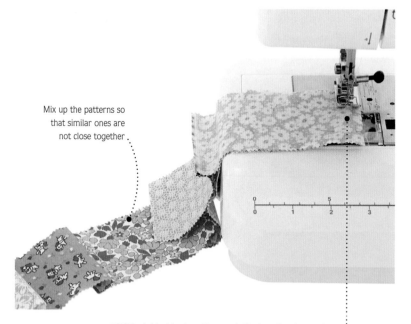

Mix up the patterns so that similar ones are not close together

4 With right sides together and aligning the short edges, stitch each paired piece to another paired piece. Make sure that the same fabrics are not next to each other. Join all the paired pieces to form one long strip.

5 Press the strip. Using the measuring tape, cut the long strip into 125cm (49in) lengths. You should have about 30 strips, depending on the amount of fabric taken up by the seams.

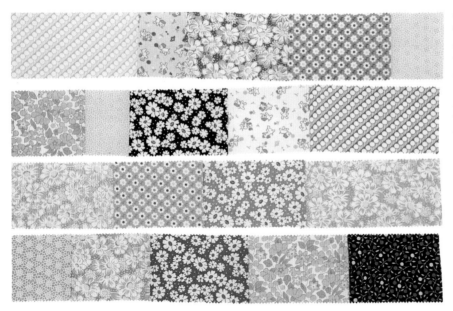

6 Lay the strips out on a large, flat surface and arrange them in a pleasing order in rows. Plan the layout of your pieces to make a quilt top that will be roughly 125 x 145cm (49 x 57in). Make sure the same fabrics are not placed together. When you are happy with the arrangement, turn each strip over and press the seams of each strip in the same direction.

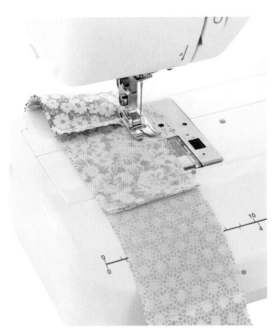

7 Working from one edge of your arrangement and with right sides together, pin the first two strips together along their length. Stitch them, leaving a 6mm (¼in) seam allowance (see p.60). Join five strips together in this way, then repeat until you have about six pieced units, each consisting of five joined strips. Your final number of pieces will depend on the number of strips you started with.

8 Pin one pieced unit to another, right sides facing, and stitch them together. Repeat until all six pieces are joined. Turn the quilt over and press the seams open. The quilt top is now complete.

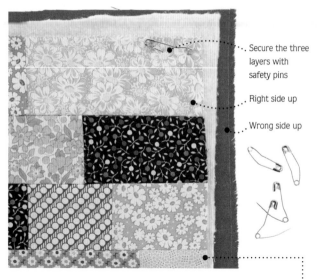

Secure the three layers with safety pins

Right side up

Wrong side up

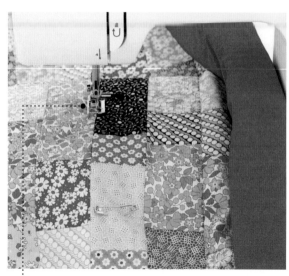

9 Piece the backing (see p.45) then lay the backing on a large, clean, flat surface with the wadding on top. Smooth out the two to make sure they are not bunched or folded, then lay the quilt top on the wadding (see p.44). The wadding and backing fabric will both extend slightly beyond the edges of the quilt top. Starting from the centre and working outwards, pin all three layers together using safety pins. Make sure that all the layers lie flat and check that the underside of the backing fabric also lies flat.

10 Quilt the top according to your preference. Here, we have quilted in the ditch (see p.135) along every sixth strip. Roll up the end of the quilt in the throat area of the sewing machine to keep it out of the way as you work (see p.134). Remove any safety pins that get in the way as you work.

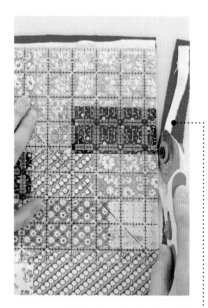

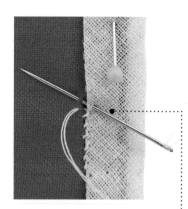

11 Using the quilter's ruler and the rotary cutter, trim away the excess wadding and backing fabric from the edges of the quilt.

12 Attach the bias tape, if used, to the edge of the quilt following the instructions on pages 48–49. Or, create a 7.5cm (3in) wide double-fold binding strip from fabric and attach it using the Double-fold binding technique on page 51.

13 Fold the binding to the back of the quilt, pin it in place, then sew it by hand slip stitching it in place (see p.49).

SIMPLE SQUARES TOTE

This cheerful tote bag is perfect for popping to the shops, heading to the beach, or carrying your quilting supplies while you are on the go. The bag is assembled using a simple, square patchwork pattern with no quilting needed.

DIFFICULTY LEVEL
Medium

SIZE
30 x 22.5 x 15cm (12 x 8¾ x 6in)

TOOLS AND MATERIALS
Measuring tape
Rotary cutter or scissors
Cutting mat (optional)
Quilter's ruler
Pins
Threads to match your fabrics
Sewing machine
Iron and ironing board
Sewing needle
One 3.5cm (1⅜in) button

FABRICS
A, B, C, D, E, F, G, H , I Assorted scraps of cotton fabric for the patchwork squares to make a total of 44 squares, each 9.5cm (3¾in)
J 50cm (20in) of 112cm (44in) wide cotton fabric for the lining
K 30cm (12in) of 112cm (44in) wide cotton fabric for the straps
L 14 x 18cm (5½ x 7in) cotton fabric for the button flap

SKILLS
Piecing (see pp.58–60)
Sewing intersecting seams (see pp.62–63)

SEAM ALLOWANCE
1cm (⅜in) throughout, unless otherwise stated

▷▷ PATTERN

FRONT AND BACK OF BAG (CUT TWO BATCHES OF 18 SQUARES)

A	B	C	D	E	G	Top row
C	H	I	F	A	H	Middle row
E	F	D	H	G	I	Bottom row

BASE OF BAG (CUT ONE BATCH OF 8 SQUARES)

A	E	B	D
H	F	I	G

Cut the patchwork squares using the diagrams as a guide to how many squares of each fabric are needed and how to lay them out. Remember to cut squares for both the front and back of the bag. You only need to cut one batch of squares for the base of the bag.

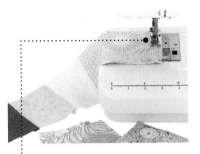

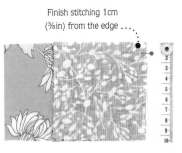

Finish stitching 1cm (⅜in) from the edge . . . .

1 Following the diagrams above, cut a total of 44 squares of fabric, each 9.5cm (3¾in) square. With right sides together, stitch together the squares for the top and middle rows of the front and back of the bag making four strips of six squares each.

2 With right sides together, stitch together the squares for the bottom row of the front and the bottom row of the back of the bag. Mark with a pin 1cm (⅜in) from the lower edge of the first and last squares in each row and take care not to sew beyond the pins.

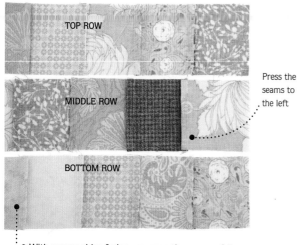

TOP ROW

MIDDLE ROW

Press the seams to the left

BOTTOM ROW

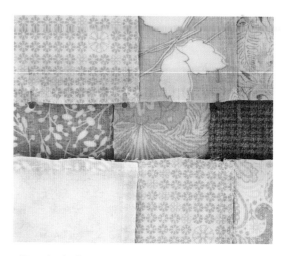

3 With wrong sides facing up, press the seams of the top and bottom rows to the right, and of the middle row to the left.

4 To make the front, with right sides together, pin, then stitch the top and middle rows together, matching the seams (see p.62). Pin and stitch the bottom row to the middle row in the same way. Repeat to make the back. Press the seams of the front downwards and the seams of the back upwards.

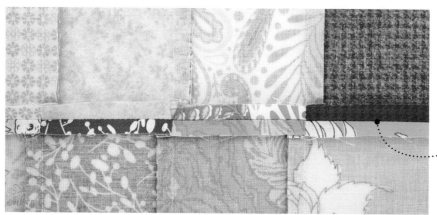

Press open the seam joining the two rows

5 With right sides together, stitch together the squares for the base in two rows of four squares. Pin, then stitch the two rows together, matching the seams. With the wrong side facing up, press this seam open.

Do not sew beyond the first and last pins

6 With right sides together, pin the lower edge of the front of the bag to one long edge of the base, matching the centre seams. Sew together, taking care not to sew beyond the pins marked in Step 2. Stitch the lower edge of the back of the bag to the other long edge of the base in the same way. Press the seams away from the base.

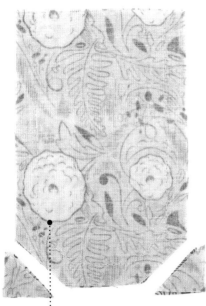

7 Cut a pair of button flaps from fabric L using the template (see p.214). With right sides together, pin, then stitch them together, leaving the upper edge open. Clip the corners as shown above.

8 Turn the flap to the right side and press. Stitch a buttonhole in the flap, large enough to accommodate your chosen button (see p.140).

9 Cut two 90 x 9cm (36 x 3½in) strips of fabric K to make the straps. With right sides together, fold the strips in half lengthwise and pin the raw edges together. Stitch, then turn to the right side and press.

10 With right sides together, pin the open edge of the flap to the centre of the upper edge of the back of the bag, and pin the end of each strap 5.5cm (2¼in) either side of the flap. Tack all the raw edges together.

11 With right sides together, fold the bag in half along the centre seam of the base. Pin both sides of the front and back of the bag together, matching the seams. Stitch the sides together, then press the seams open.

12 Bring the raw lower edges of the front and back of the bag to meet the short edges of the base. Match the bag's side seams to the centre seam of the base. Pin, then stitch between the ends of the seams that were sewn in Step 6. Turn the bag to the right side.

MAKE THE LINING

Leave a 16cm (6¼in)
gap on one side edge

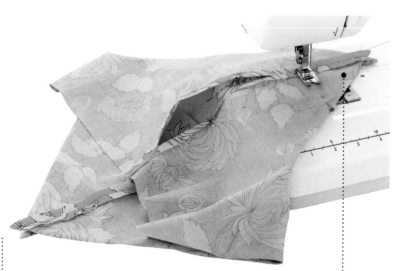

13 Cut two 47 x 32cm (18¾ x 12¾in) rectangles of lining fabric. Pin them together with right sides facing. Stitch along one long side – the bottom edge – and along the two short sides, leaving a 16cm (6¼in) opening along one short side, 4cm (1½in) from the upper edge.

14 To shape the lining to fit the base of the bag, with right sides of the lining facing, bring the lower part of one side seam to the adjacent part of the seam along the bottom of the lining. Starting at the corner where these seams intersect, measure and mark a point 15cm (6in) away. Sew across the lining, perpendicular to this mark, creating a triangle at the corner. Repeat on the opposite side of the lining.

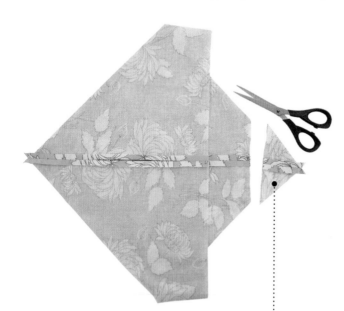

15 Trim the seam allowances to 1cm (⅜in) and cut off the triangles, as shown.

16 Insert the bag into the lining with right sides facing. Pin the upper raw edges together, matching the side seams. Remove the base of the sewing machine, then slip the bag over the sewing machine bed and stitch along the upper edge.

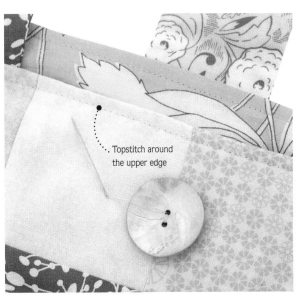

17 Turn the bag to the right side through the opening in the side of the lining. Slip stitch (see p.41) the opening in the lining closed. Press the lining to the inside.

Topstitch around the upper edge

18 Topstitch the bag 6mm (¼in) below the upper edge to keep the lining inside the bag. Sew the button to the centre seam of the top row of patchwork on the front of the bag, 4cm (1½in) below the upper edge.

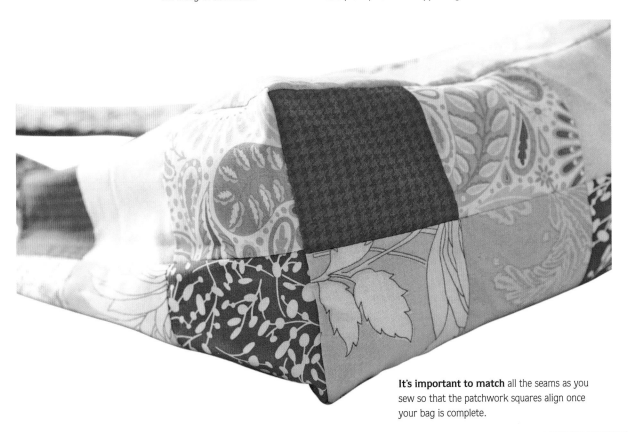

It's important to match all the seams as you sew so that the patchwork squares align once your bag is complete.

TRIANGLE FLOOR CUSHION

This floor cushion will show off your patchworking skills. It is easier to make than you may think, since it involves repeating the same techniques and building up the pattern a little at a time. It's simple to substitute colours and fabrics of your choice.

DIFFICULTY LEVEL
Medium

SIZE
65 x 65cm (26 x 26in)

TOOLS AND MATERIALS
Tracing paper
Marker pen
Pins
Quilter's ruler
Scissors
Rotary cutter
Cutting mat
Threads to match your fabrics
Sewing machine
Iron and ironing board
Contrast thread for tacking
Sewing needle
51cm (20in) zip
65cm (26in) square cushion pad

FABRICS
80 x 112cm (31½ x 44in) blue cotton
    fabric
40 x 112cm (16 x 44in) aqua cotton fabric
20 x 112cm (8 x 44in) pale green
    cotton fabric
20 x 112cm (8 x 44in) jade green
    cotton fabric

SKILLS
Sewing triangles (see pp.64-65)
Sashings and borders (see pp.78-83)

SEAM ALLOWANCE
1cm (⅜in) throughout, unless
    otherwise stated

TIP
Match the points of the sashings
    for a professional finish.

⏩ PATTERN

CUSHION LAYOUT

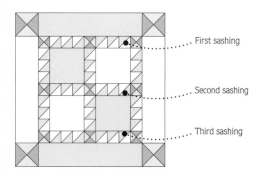

First sashing

Second sashing

Third sashing

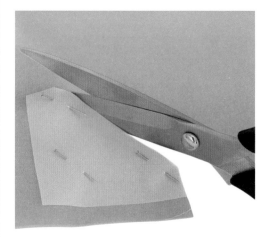

Pair the blue and aqua triangles and chain piece along the diagonal edge .

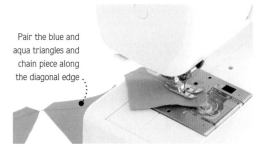

1 Trace the templates (see p.214) onto the tracing paper and cut them out. From each of the blue and aqua fabrics, cut 36 medium triangles, two 17cm (6¾in) squares, and two 47 x 12cm (18¾ x 4¾in) rectangles for the borders. From each of the pale green and jade green fabrics, cut 18 small triangles and eight large triangles. Cut two 67 x 35cm (26¾ x 14in) rectangles from the blue fabric; these are the two back pieces of the cushion cover.

2 With right sides together, pair up a medium blue triangle with a medium aqua triangle. Chain piece them together (see p.61) along the long, diagonal edges, leaving a 1cm (⅜in) seam allowance.

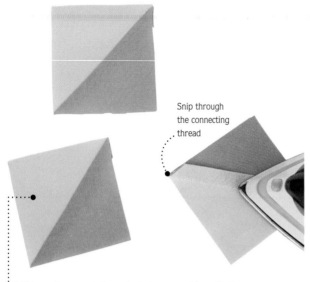

Snip through
the connecting
thread

3 Using scissors, cut the paired pieces apart by snipping through the short length of thread between them. Press the seams towards the darker triangles. You will have 36 half-square triangles.

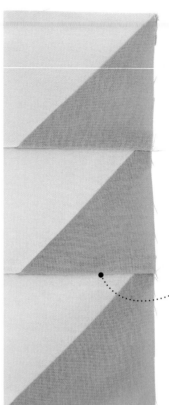

4 Lay three of the half-square triangles in a vertical row with the aqua triangles on the left-hand side. With right sides together, stitch the half-square triangles together, leaving a 1cm (⅜in) seam allowance. Press the seams towards the darker triangles. Repeat to make a total of six rows. These are the vertical sashings.

Press the seams towards
the darker triangles

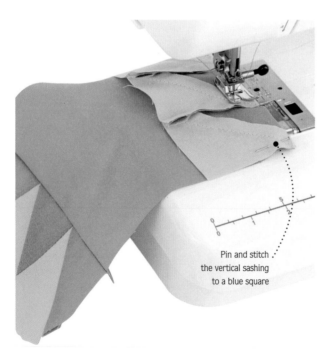

Pin and stitch
the vertical sashing
to a blue square

5 With right sides together, pin a vertical sashing to each of the two opposite sides of a blue square so the blue triangles of the sashing adjoin the blue square. Stitch, leaving a 1cm (⅜in) seam allowance, then press the seams towards the square.

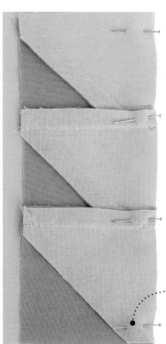

6 With right sides together, pin a vertical sashing to the right-hand edge of an aqua square so the aqua triangles of the sashing adjoin the aqua square. Stitch, leaving a 1cm (⅜in) seam allowance, then press the seams towards the square.

Pin and stitch
the vertical sashing
to an aqua square

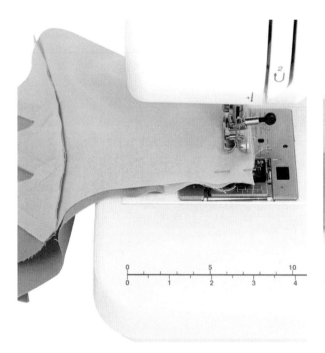

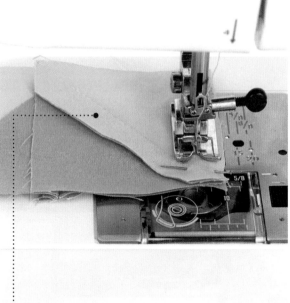

7 With right sides together and the sashings vertical, pin the left-hand raw edge of the aqua square to one of the vertical sashings attached to the blue square. Stitch, leaving a 1cm (⅜in) seam allowance. Press towards the aqua square. Repeat Steps 5–7 to join the other blue and aqua squares in the same way, to make two patchwork rectangles.

8 To make the horizontal sashings, lay three of the remaining 18 half-square triangles in a horizontal row with the aqua triangles along the top edge. With right sides together, stitch the half-square triangles together, leaving a 1cm (⅜in) seam allowance. Press the seams towards the darker triangles. Repeat to make a total of six horizontal sashings.

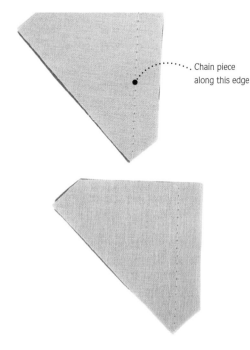

Chain piece along this edge

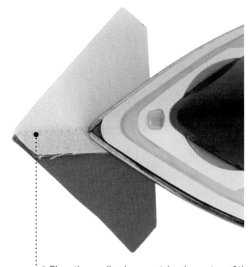

9 Place the small pale green triangles on top of the small jade green triangles with the points of the triangles top right, as shown. Chain piece the triangles together along the right-hand edges, leaving a 1cm (⅜in) seam allowance. Snip the triangles apart. Press the seams towards the jade green triangles.

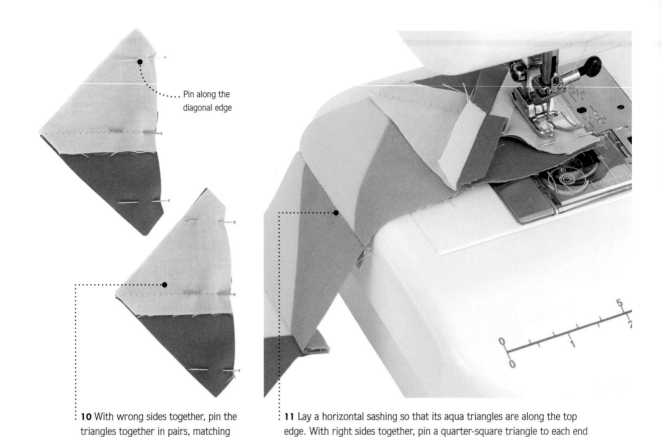

Pin along the
diagonal edge

10 With wrong sides together, pin the triangles together in pairs, matching the seams. Chain piece them together as in Step 9. Snip them apart, then open them to form nine small quarter-square triangles. Press the seams open.

11 Lay a horizontal sashing so that its aqua triangles are along the top edge. With right sides together, pin a quarter-square triangle to each end of the sashing, so the small pale green triangles adjoin the sashing. Stitch, leaving a 1cm (⅜in) seam allowance. Press the seams towards the quarter-square triangles.

Pin the second horizontal
sashing to the first one,
right sides together

Stitch and unfold

12 Lay another horizontal sashing so that its aqua triangles are along the bottom edge. With right sides together, pin it to the right-hand edge (a small pale green triangle) of the quarter-square triangle that was attached in Step 11. Stitch, leaving a 1cm (⅜in)

seam allowance. Press the seams towards the quarter-square triangles. Repeat steps 11–12 to complete another horizontal sashing. You now have the first and third sashings.

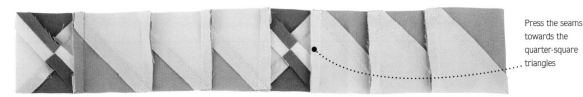

Press the seams towards the quarter-square triangles

13 To make the second sashing, lay one of the remaining horizontal sashings horizontally right side up, with the blue triangles along the top edge. With right sides together, pin a quarter-square triangle to each end of the sashing, so the small pale green triangles adjoin the sashing. Pin the aqua triangle at the end of the remaining horizontal sashing to the small pale green triangle on the right-hand edge of the quarter-square triangle. Stitch, leaving a 1cm (⅜in) seam allowance. Press the seams towards the small quarter-square triangles.

14 With right sides together and leaving a 1cm (⅜in) seam allowance, pin and stitch the small pale green triangles of the remaining three quarter-square triangles to the raw ends of all three horizontal sashings. Press the seams towards the quarter-square triangles. Note: the image shows the final quarter-square triangle being pinned to either the first or third horizontal sashing.

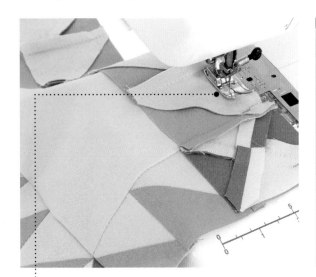

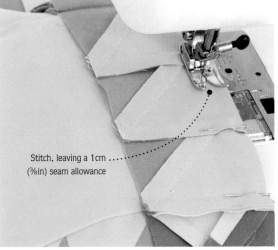

Stitch, leaving a 1cm (⅜in) seam allowance

15 With right sides together, pin the first and second horizontal sashings to the long edges of one of the patchwork rectangles made in Step 7. Place the blue triangles so they adjoin the blue square and the aqua triangles so they adjoin the aqua square. Stitch, matching seams and leaving a 1cm (⅜in) seam allowance. Press the seams away from the sashings.

16 With right sides together, pin the lower edge of the second sashing and one long edge of the third sashing to the long edges of the remaining patchwork rectangle. Place the aqua triangles so they adjoin the aqua square and the blue triangles so they adjoin the blue square. Stitch, matching seams and leaving a 1cm (⅜in) seam allowance. Press the seams away from the sashings. The centre block of the cushion cover is now complete.

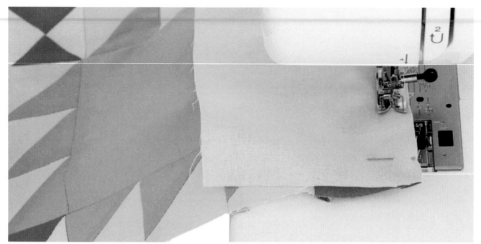

17 With right sides together, pin and stitch an aqua border to each of the two opposite sides of the centre block, leaving a 1cm (⅜in) seam allowance. Press the seams towards the borders.

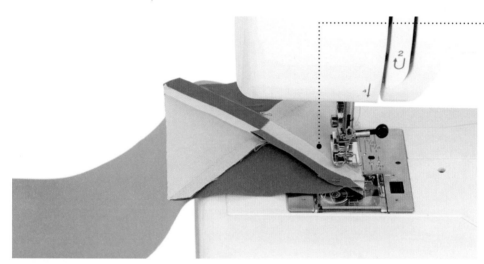

18 Using the large pale green and jade green triangles and following Steps 9 and 10, make four large quarter-square triangles. With right sides together, pin one quarter-square triangle to each end of the two blue borders, matching the pale green triangles to the short edges. Stitch the short edges, leaving a 1cm (⅜in) seam allowance. Press the seams towards the borders.

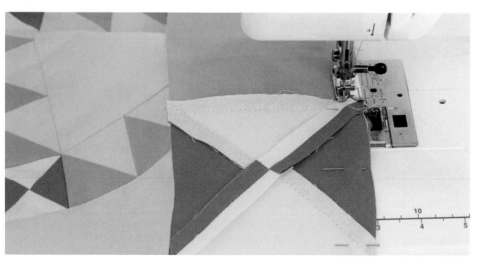

19 With right sides together and matching the seams, pin the blue borders to the centre block and their attached quarter-square triangles to the short edges of the aqua borders. Stitch, leaving a 1cm (⅜in) seam allowance. Press the seams towards the borders and the large quarter-square triangles. The front of the cushion cover is now complete.

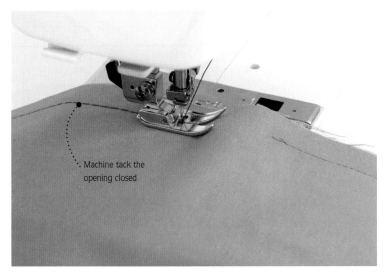

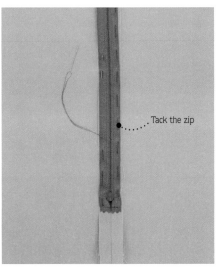

20 With right sides together, pin and stitch the back pieces of the cushion together along one long edge, leaving a 1.5cm (⅝in) seam allowance and a 51cm (20in) opening at the centre. Tack the opening closed by machine or by hand. Press the seam open.

21 On the wrong side of the back, pin and hand tack the zip, face down, in the centre of the opening (see p.141).

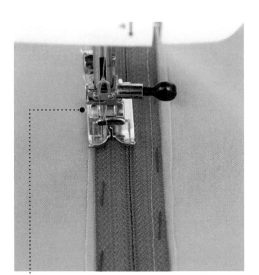

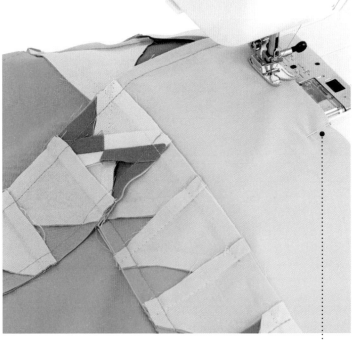

22 On the wrong side, use a zipper foot to stitch around the zip, 6mm (¼in) from the edges of the zip, and straight across the ends. Remove the tacking stitches. Undo the zip in readiness for turning the cushion cover to the right side.

23 With right sides together, pin the front and back of the cushion cover together. Stitch around the outer edge, leaving a 1cm (⅜in) seam allowance. Turn the cushion cover to the right side, insert the cushion pad, and close the zip.

DIAMOND COASTERS

These coasters can be whipped up in no time and are perfect for practising set-in-seams. They can easily be made from odd scraps of fabric that you might have around the house. Make them as a house-warming gift – or to keep for yourself.

DIFFICULTY LEVEL
Easy

SIZE
11.5cm (4½in) diameter approximately

TOOLS AND MATERIALS
Tracing paper
Pencil
Scissors
Quilter's ruler
Rotary cutter
Cutting mat
Sewing machine
Threads to match your fabrics
Pins
Sewing needle

FABRICS
Three 15 x 9cm (6 x 3½in) pieces of
    coordinating fabric scraps per coaster
15 x 15cm (6 x 6in) backing fabric
15 x 15cm (6 x 6in) wadding (optional)

LAVENDER BAG VARIATION
16cm (6¼in) of thin ribbon
Dried lavender

SKILLS
Set-in seams (see p.75)

SEAM ALLOWANCE
6mm (¼in) throughout, unless
    otherwise stated

▷ PATTERN

1 Trace the diamond template (see p.214) onto the tracing paper and cut out the diamond pattern piece. Be sure to add the 6mm (¼in) seam allowance lines to the pattern piece. Place the pattern piece on a piece of scrap fabric and, using the quilter's ruler and the rotary cutter, cut a fabric diamond. When cutting, align the marked seam allowance with the 6mm (¼in) mark on the quilter's ruler to ensure that you do not make the pattern piece smaller each time you cut.

2 To prepare to sew set-in seams (see p.75), mark a dot 6mm (¼in) inside each corner on the back of each fabric diamond. Pin two diamonds, right sides together, along one edge. Sew the diamonds together between the two marked dots, taking care not to sew beyond the dots.

3 Following the same technique, set in the third diamond to complete the coaster top. Press the seams at the back to one side.

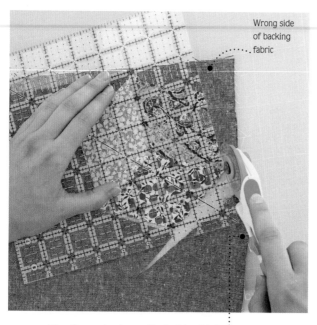

Wrong side
of backing
fabric

4 Lay the coaster top on the backing fabric.
Using the quilter's ruler and the rotary cutter,
cut a piece of the backing fabric to match.

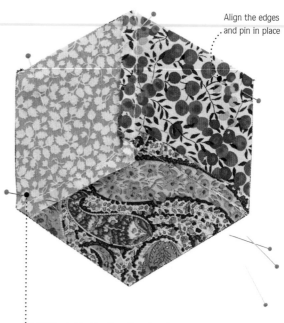

Align the edges
and pin in place

5 With right sides together, lay the coaster top
on the backing fabric. Align the edges and pin
all around.

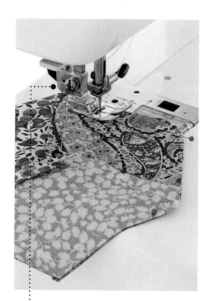

6 Sew around the edges, leaving an
opening of approximately 5cm (2in)
along one edge for turning through.

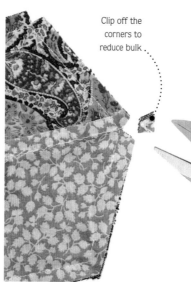

Clip off the
corners to
reduce bulk

7 Clip into each corner, taking care
not to cut through the stitches.

8 Turn the coaster to the right side through
the opening and pick out the corners with
a pin. Iron thoroughly. If you would like a
more padded and absorbent coaster, cut a
piece of wadding smaller than the coaster
and insert it through the opening. Press
the wadding flat.

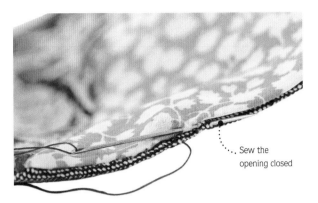

Sew the opening closed

9 Oversew (see p.41) the opening in the edge of the coaster closed, picking up a few threads from each side of the opening as you go.

10 Leaving a 1cm (⅜in) seam allowance, topstitch around the edges of the coaster with coordinating thread. You can quilt the coaster in any pattern you wish to help hold the wadding in place, if used.

⫸ LAVENDER BAG VARIATION

By slightly altering the pattern, you can turn the coaster into a lavender bag for your wardrobe to keep moths at bay. You can also make the lavender bag without a ribbon and use it as a scented sachet to keep in a drawer.

1 Follow Steps 1–4 of the coaster. At Step 5, pin the length of ribbon between the coaster top and the backing. Centre the ribbon on one corner. Complete Steps 6–8 of the coaster, securing the ends of the ribbon in place in Step 6.

2 Stuff the lavender bag with dried lavender, then sew up the opening in the edge, as in Step 9 of the coaster. Your lavender bag is now complete.

Keep moths at bay in your wardrobe by looping these pretty patchwork lavender bags on your clothes hangers. Thanks to the natural properties of lavender, the bags will act as moth-repellents.

SIMPLE SASHINGS CUSHION

A simple block pattern framed by sashing can be an attractive addition to any chair in the room. If using fabrics with a directional pattern, be sure to cut and sew them so that they're the correct way up on the cushion front.

DIFFICULTY LEVEL
Easy

SIZE
40 x 40cm (16 x 16in)

TOOLS AND MATERIALS
Rotary cutter
Cutting mat
Quilter's ruler
Pins
Thread to match your fabrics
Sewing machine
Scissors
40cm (16in) square cushion pad

FABRICS
A 28 x 28cm (11 x 11in) patterned flower fabric
B 28 x 28cm (11 x 11in) patterned dotty fabric
C 6.5 x 6.5cm (2½ x 2½in) patterned bird fabric
D 13 x 13cm (5 x 5in) patterned triangle fabric
E 60 x 70cm (23½ x 27½in) solid grey fabric
F 10 x 26cm (4 x 10in) patterned fabric, for the back inset detail

SKILLS
Sashing and borders (see pp.78–83)

SEAM ALLOWANCE
1cm (⅜in) seam allowance throughout, unless otherwise stated

▶ PATTERN

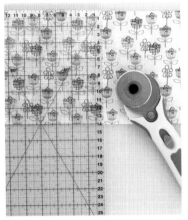

1 Cut four 14cm (5½in) squares from fabric A; four 6.5 x 14cm (2½ x 5½in) strips from fabric B (if you are using a directional pattern for the sashing you will need to cut two strips with the pattern across the width of the strip and two strips with the pattern across the height of the strip); four 6.5cm (2½in) squares from fabric D; four 6.5 x 32cm (2½ x 12½in) strips (cutting two strips with the pattern across the width of the strip and two strips with the pattern across the height of the strip); one 42 x 26cm (16½ x 10in) rectangle; one 12 x 26cm (4½ x 10in) rectangle; and one 22 x 26cm (8½ x 10in) rectangle from fabric E.

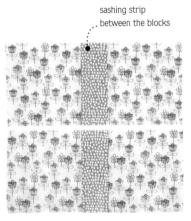

Set the vertical sashing strip between the blocks

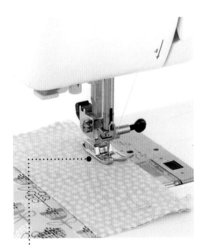

2 Lay out all your pieces for the cushion front on a flat surface. With right sides together, pin and sew the first fabric B strip (with the pattern running height-wise to the first fabric A square). Open up the seam and sew the second fabric A square to the opposite side of the strip.

3 Repeat using the second height-wise fabric B strip and the remaining two fabric A squares to create the two front strips. Ensure that all of the patterns on the fabrics are running the same way – in this case that all the flowers are upright. Open up and press the seams towards the darker fabric.

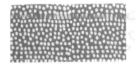

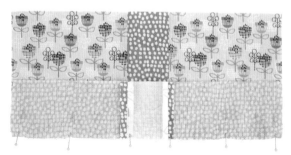

.·. Make sure the sashing strip is straight – trim if needed

4 Take the two remaining fabric B strips and the fabric C square and sew them together with the square in the centre to create the central sashing. Press the seams open.

5 Pin and sew the central sashing to the bottom edge of the top front strip, being sure to match the seams on all the pieces (see p.62). Make sure that when the strip is sewn and opened up that the pattern is the same way up on all the pieces.

6 Pin and sew the bottom front strip to the bottom edge of the central sashing, matching the seams as you pin. Ensure all of the patterns are the right way up. Press open the seams to create the main cushion front.

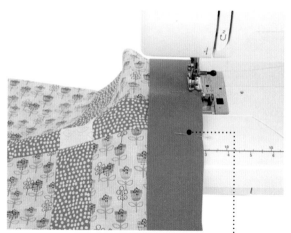

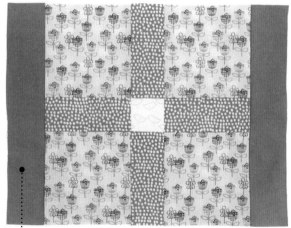

7 Pin and sew one of the fabric E strips with the pattern running height-wise to the right edge of the main cushion front, right sides together.

8 Pin and sew the second height-wise fabric E strip to the left edge of the main cushion front. Open out and press the seams just sewn towards the darker fabrics.

9 Sew two fabric D squares to either end of one of the remaining fabric E strips, as shown, to create the first border. Repeat using the remaining two fabric D squares and final fabric E strip to create the second border. Press the seams towards the darker fabric.

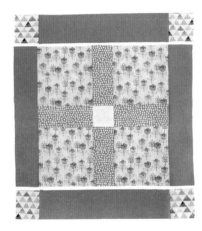

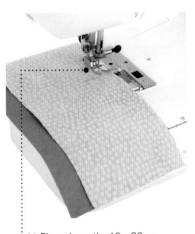

Fold the long edge twice
to create a neat hem

10 Pin and sew the two borders to the top and bottom of the main cushion front, matching the seams and ensuring all of the patterns are the right way up. Press the seams open.

11 Pin and sew the 10 x 26cm (4 x 10in) fabric F rectangle right sides together with the 12 x 26cm (4½ x 10in) fabric E rectangle. Pin and sew the 22 x 26cm (8½ x 10in) fabric E rectangle to the opposite side of the fabric F rectangle to create a 42 x 26cm (16½ x 10in) strip.

12 You now have two 42 x 26cm (16½ x 10in) strips – one plain and one with a strip of fabric F running through it – these are the back flaps. Turn over one of the long raw edges of one flap by 1cm (⅜in) to the wrong side using a seam guide if needed, then the same again to create a hem. Pin in place. Repeat on the second flap.

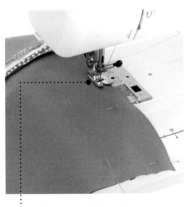

13 Using a matching thread, topstitch along the inner fold to secure the hem. Repeat on the second flap.

14 Lay the cushion front out, right side up. Then lay the plain back flap on top, right side down, with the raw edges aligning with the top of the cushion front. Lay the second flap on top of this, right side down, with the raw edges aligning with the raw edges of the bottom of the cushion front. Pin all around.

15 Stitch around the entire perimeter of the cushion. Forward and reverse stitch over the area where the flaps overlap to reinforce the seam. Carefully snip off all four corners being sure not to cut through any of the stitches. Turn the cushion cover right side out, carefully pushing out the corners and insert the cushion pad.

DRESDEN PLATE CUSHION

This round cushion features a traditional Dresden plate patchwork block. Many variations of the Dresden plate block exist, but this one is a multi-petalled flower. Once the "plate" is complete, it is hand-sewn to the front of the cushion.

DIFFICULTY LEVEL
Medium

SIZE
38cm (15in) in diameter x 10cm (4in) deep

TOOLS AND MATERIALS
Tracing paper
Measuring tape
Pencil
Pins
Threads to match your fabrics
Sewing machine
Scissors
Iron and ironing board
Sewing needle

FABRICS
50 x 85cm (20 x 33½in) plain white fabric for the circle for the cushion front and for the two semicircles for the cushion back
A selection of seven patterned blue fabrics for the petals and the flower centre
24 x 62cm (9½ x 24½in) blue fabric, cut into two rectangles, each 12 x 62cm (4¾ x 24½in) for the cushion sides
Toy filling, wadding, or a 38cm (15in) diameter x 10cm (4in) deep round cushion pad

SKILLS
Chain piecing (see p.61)
Curves and fans (see pp.84–85)

SEAM ALLOWANCE
6mm (¼in) throughout, unless otherwise stated

▷▷ PATTERN

1 Using the template on page 215, cut two petals from each of six differently patterned blue fabrics, giving a total of 12 petals. Arrange the petals in a circle, with matching petals directly opposite each other, as shown. Cut the remaining pieces for the cushion using the templates and instructions on page 215.

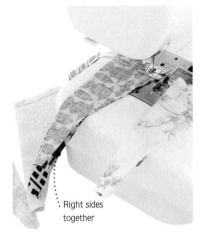

Right sides together

2 Fold the wider end of each petal in half, right side to right side, and pin. Chain piece all the petals together (see p.61).

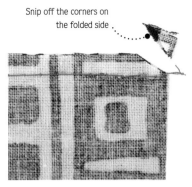

Snip off the corners on the folded side

3 Cut the petals apart and snip off the inside, folded corner of each petal.

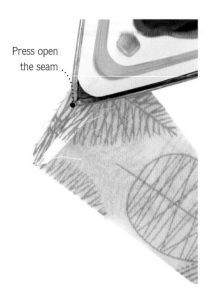

Press open
the seam

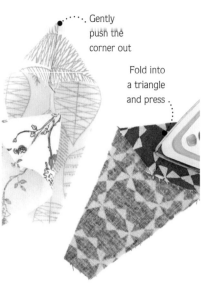

Gently
push the
corner out

Fold into
a triangle
and press

Start stitching
from here

4 Press the seams open using an iron or finger press.

5 Turn each petal to the right side and gently push the corner out. Fold the wider end of the petal to the wrong side to form a symmetrical triangle. Press in place. Lay the petals out in the correct order again.

6 Pin two adjacent petals together, right sides together, along the long edge. Starting at the triangular end, stitch along the edge. Stop stitching 6mm (¼in) from the narrow end of the petals. Press the seam open.

Fold the narrow ends
to the wrong side
and tack in place

7 Continue adding the remaining petals in the same way, pressing the seams open as you go, until you have a full circle or "plate" of joined petals.

8 Fold over 6mm (¼in) of the narrow ends of the petals to the wrong side of the fabric, then press and tack.

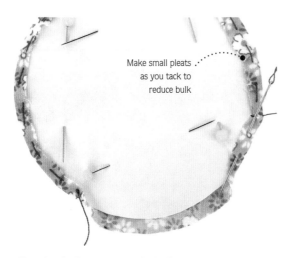

Make small pleats
as you tack to
reduce bulk

Measure from the
edge of the circle to
the tip of each petal
to check that the
petals are centred

9 To make the flower centre, pin the flower centre pattern piece to the wrong side of the flower centre fabric. Fold the seam allowance over the pattern piece and tack together, making small pleats in the fabric to reduce the bulk. Press to set the pleats.

10 Lay the white circle of fabric for the front, right side up. Measure and mark the centre, then place the completed "plate" of petals on top, right side up and centred. Measure from the edge of the circle to the tip of each petal to ensure the petals are centred.

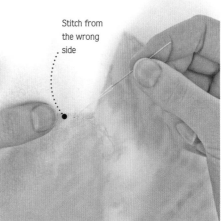

Stitch from
the wrong
side

11 Pin the plate in place along its inside and outside edges. As you pin, make sure that the mark in the centre of the white circle remains in the centre of the plate and that the tips of the petals remain equidistant from the edge of the white circle.

12 Using small slip stitches and matching thread (see p.41), and working from the wrong side, sew the outside and inside edges of the plate to the white circle, making the stitches as invisible as possible.

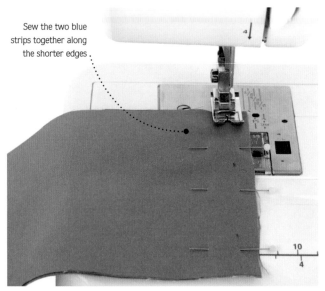

Sew the two blue strips together along the shorter edges

13 To complete the cushion front, unpick the tacking stitches from the flower centre and gently remove the paper pattern piece. Pin the wrong side of the flower centre to the centre of the plate. Slip stitch in place.

14 To make the sides of the cushion, place the two blue strips right sides together. Pin their shorter edges together at both ends, then sew them together, leaving a 1cm (⅜in) seam allowance. Press the seams open. You will now have a loop of fabric.

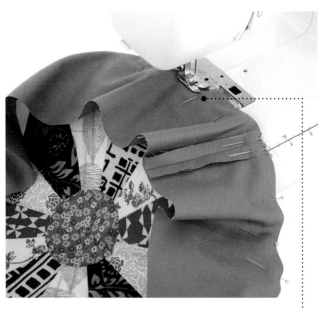

Pin the blue strip around the edge

15 With right sides together, pin one long edge of the blue loop all around the edge of the cushion front.

16 Sew all around the pinned edge, leaving a 1cm (⅜in) seam allowance.

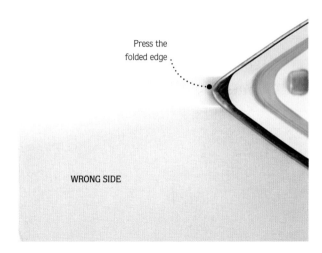

Press the folded edge

WRONG SIDE

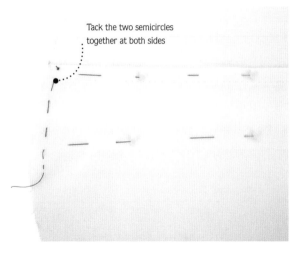

Tack the two semicircles together at both sides

17 To make the back of the cushion, lay out the bigger white semicircle wrong side up. Fold the straight edge over by 1cm (⅜in) and press, then fold it over again to create a neat hem and to enclose the raw edge. Press again, then topstitch together. Repeat on the straight edge of the smaller semicircle.

18 With right sides face up and with the larger semicircle on top, lay the two semicircles together to form a full circle. Overlap the hemmed edges by about 4.5cm (1⅝in). Pin along both sides of the overlap, then tack the two overlapped semicircles together at both sides, inside the 1cm (⅜in) seam allowance. Remove the pins along the overlapped edges.

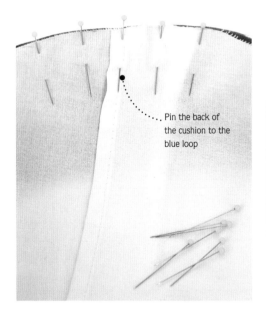

Pin the back of the cushion to the blue loop

Turn the cushion to the right side through the opening

19 With right sides together, pin the back of the cushion to the remaining long edge of the blue loop. Remove the tacking stitches from the back of the cushion, then sew all around the pinned edge, leaving a 1cm (⅜in) seam allowance.

20 Turn the cushion to the right side through the opening in the back and press the seams that join the sides of the cushion to the front and back. Stuff the cushion with toy filling, wadding, or a cushion pad.

ELECTRONIC DEVICE COVER

You can make this project to fit any electronic device, whether it's a laptop, tablet, or even a phone. Just remember to adjust all of the fabric requirements and flower template size, as needed. You can use a paper clip to hold the template and fabric pieces together.

DIFFICULTY LEVEL
Medium

SIZE
To fit the device of your choice

TOOLS AND MATERIALS
Card
Paper clip (optional)
Pins
Needle
Threads to match the fabrics
Quilter's ruler
Cutting mat
Rotary cutter
Tailor's chalk or water-soluble pen
Scissors
Velcro® for the closure. You will need enough to fit across the width of your device

FABRICS
12 x 18cm (5 x 7 in) petal fabric
6 x 6cm (2½ x 2½ in) flower centre fabric
Calculate the main fabric requirements for your device by following the instructions in Step 4
You will need enough wadding to fit around the circumference of your device, plus 15.5cm (6in) extra in both dimensions
Bias tape to fit the edges of your device ([length + height of device] x 2)

SKILLS
English paper piecing (see pp.88–89)

SEAM ALLOWANCE
6mm (¼in), unless otherwise stated

▶▶ PATTERN

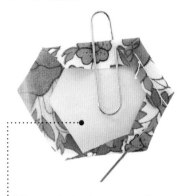

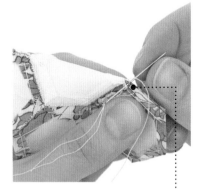

1 Copy and cut out seven paper hexagons using the template on page 214. Using the English paper piecing technique (see p.88) create six hexagons in the petal fabric and one hexagon from the flower centre fabric.

2 Join the hexagons into a flower shape, oversewing the petals to the centre hexagon, then the sides of the petals to one another (see p.88).

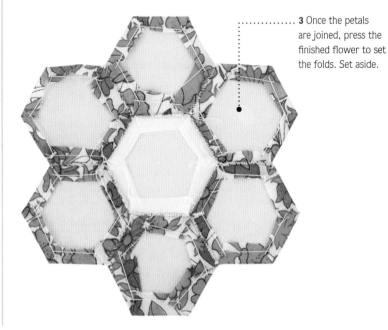

3 Once the petals are joined, press the finished flower to set the folds. Set aside.

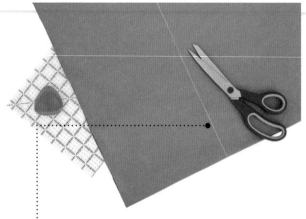

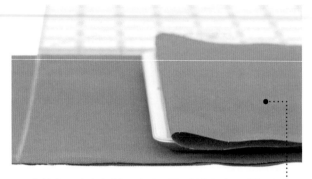

4 Measure the circumference of the width of your device, divide by two, then add 2.5cm (1in) to the total. Then, measure the circumference of the height of your device, add 15.5cm (6in), then multiply by two. Measure and cut a strip of fabric with these dimensions.

5 Fold the strip in half lengthwise. The folded edge will be the top, front edge of the cover. Place the device on the strip and then fold the folded edge up and over the front of the device so that it sits just below the top edge of the device, as shown. Measure and mark a line approximately 6.5cm (2½in), or the length of your choice, from the top of the device to create the flap. Cut along the line just marked. Mark a second line where the top of the device sits.

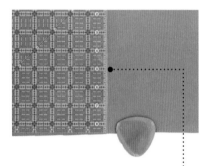

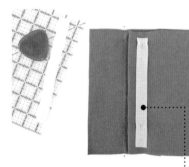

6 Open up the fabric strip and measure and mark a line in the centre of the fabric, where it was previously folded.

7 Cut a piece of wadding to fit on one half of the fabric strip, from the halfway line just marked to the opposite edge. Trim it slightly smaller all around so that it sits just inside the edges of the fabric. Fold the other side of fabric lengthwise over the wadding, on the marked line, aligning all of the edges.

8 Fold the folded edge of the strip up to just below the line that marks the top of the device. Pin on the line. Cut a piece of Velcro® slightly shorter than the width of the fabric strip. Pin the rough side of the Velcro® just below the folded edge, on the front.

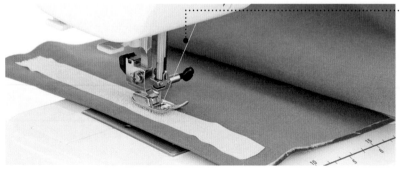

9 Using a matching thread, topstitch around all four edges of the rough Velcro® piece to attach it to the front of the cover.

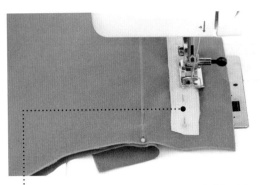

10 Pin the soft side of the Velcro® to the inside of the flap, only through the inside piece of fabric and wadding, so that when the flap is folded over the two halves of Velcro® will meet one another. Place your device inside the roughly constructed cover to ensure the placement is correct. Topstitch the piece of Velcro® in place being sure not to stitch through the outer fabric flap.

11 Carefully remove the paper from your flower and pin the flower on the front of the cover, in the location of your choice.

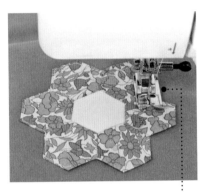

12 Using a matching thread, topstitch around the outer edges of the flower to attach it to the front of the cover only.

13 Fold the front of the cover back up in place so that the folded front edge sits just below the line. Pin around the three raw edges of the cover.

14 Starting in the bottom left corner, sew around the three raw edges using a 6mm (¼in) seam allowance.

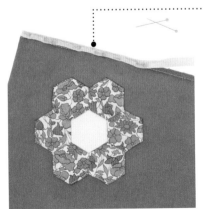

15 Pin the bias tape around the three raw edges, mitring the corners and folding under the raw edges of the bias tape at either end.

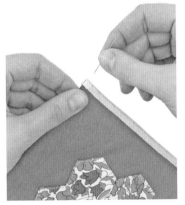

16 Using a needle and matching thread, attach the bias tape to the edges. We've used a running stitch, weaving back and forth through all the layers at one time.

LOG CABIN CUSHION

This cushion uses four log cabin blocks, each with light fabrics radiating from one corner, and dark fabrics from the other. This light and dark contrast is traditional in log cabin blocks, and the greater the contrast, the more dramatic the effect.

DIFFICULTY LEVEL
Easy

SIZE
40 x 40cm (16 x 16in)

TOOLS AND MATERIALS
Rotary cutter
Cutting mat
Quilter's ruler
Pins
Sewing machine
Threads to match your fabrics
Iron and ironing board
Curved safety pins or a sewing needle
Scissors

FABRICS
A 9 x 9cm (3½ x 3½in) centre fabric
B 9 x 9cm (3½ x 3½in) red fabric
C 18 x 7cm (7 x 2¾in) red fabric
D 18 x 7cm (7 x 2¾in) white fabric
E 18 x 10.5cm (7 x 4¼in) white fabric
F 18 x 10.5cm (7 x 4¼in) red fabric
G 18 x 14cm (7 x 5½in) red fabric
H 18 x 14cm (7 x 5½in) white fabric
I 18 x 17.5cm (7 x 6¾in) white fabric
J 18 x 17.5cm (7 x 6¾in) red fabric
K 18 x 21cm (7 x 8½in) red fabric
L 18 x 21cm (7 x 8½in) grey fabric
M 18 x 24.5cm (7 x 9½in) black fabric
46cm x 100cm (18 x 39in) backing fabric
42 x 42cm (16½ x 16½in) wadding
40cm (16in) square cushion pad

SKILLS
Log cabin (see pp.92–93)

SEAM ALLOWANCE
6mm (¼in) throughout, unless otherwise stated

▶▶ PATTERN

Make sure the fabric aligns on all four edges ....

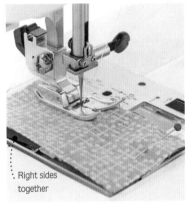
Right sides together

1 Cut your fabric pieces to size, starting with a 4.5cm (1¾in) square for the centre of each block. Cut each strip to 4.5cm (1¾in) wide by the required length (see p.35).

2 Create a block following the instructions on page 92. With right sides together, join piece A to piece B, then continue adding the pieces in order until the block is complete. Press the seams as you work (see pp.42–43).

3 Repeat to create four identical blocks. Use your quilter's ruler to square up the block and trim off any uneven or untidy edges.

4 Arrange the four blocks as you would like them to appear on the cushion front. Here a traditional light and dark colour contrast has been used, but you can choose any arrangement you wish for your cushion (see p.77).

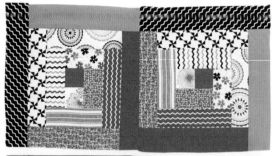

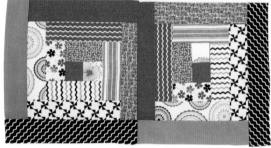

5 With right sides together, pin together, then sew the top two blocks of your design, and the bottom two blocks. Here the blocks have been joined so that the darker colours are adjacent to each other. Press the seams open.

6 To complete the cushion front, with right sides together, pin, then sew the top pair of blocks to the bottom pair of blocks. Keep the seams joining the strips aligned between one pair of blocks and the other. Press the seam open.

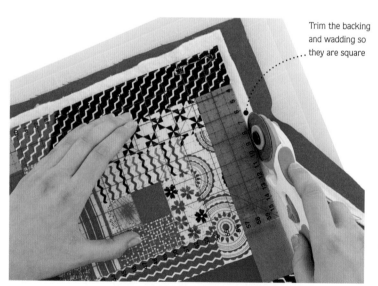

Trim the backing and wadding so they are square

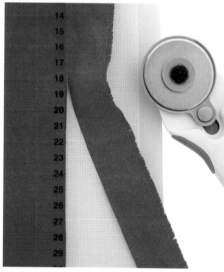

7 Lay out a piece of backing fabric and place the wadding on top. Place the cushion front on top of the wadding, right side face up. Use safety pins or tack all three layers together. Use the quilter's ruler and rotary cutter to trim the wadding and backing fabric square with the edges of the cushion front.

8 To make the cushion back, cut two pieces from the backing fabric, each 42 x 26cm (16½ x 10in). Fold one of the long edges of one piece to the wrong side of the fabric by 1cm (⅜in). Fold it again by the same amount to create a neat hem and to enclose the raw edge. Pin the hem in place.

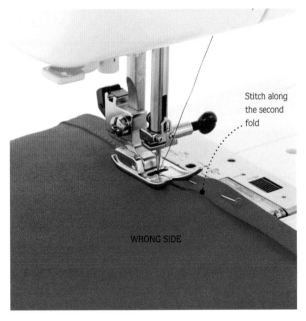

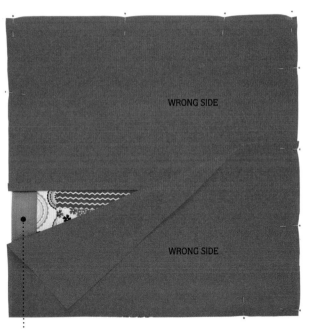

9 Check that the hem is straight, then sew along the edge of the second fold to secure the hem. Repeat Steps 8 and 9 on the other piece of fabric to make the second back piece.

10 Lay the cushion front, right side up. Place one of the back pieces on top, right side down, aligning its long, unhemmed edge with the top raw edge of the cushion front. Place the second back piece right side down on top of the first, aligning its long, unhemmed edge with the bottom raw edge of the cushion front. The two cushion back pieces should overlap. Pin along all four edges.

11 Leaving a 1cm (⅜in) seam allowance, sew around all four edges of the cushion cover to secure the back pieces to the cushion front. Remove the pins as you work.

12 Snip off all four corners, taking care not to cut through the stitches. Turn the cushion cover to the right side through the opening in the back. Iron and insert the cushion pad.

CHEVRON QUILT

Create a visually appealing chevron pattern by using bold, contrasting fabrics for the stripes, or choose similar colours for a more subtle quilt.

You can try adding more rows, for more chevrons, or even fill the entire quilt top with chevrons.

DIFFICULTY LEVEL
Medium

SIZE
98 x 135cm (38½ x 53in)

TOOLS AND MATERIALS
Measuring tape
Quilter's ruler
Rotary cutter
Cutting mat
Scissors
Sewing machine
Threads to match your fabrics
Iron and ironing board
Safety pins
Pins
Sewing needle

FABRICS
A 44 x 112cm (17 x 44in) white fabric
B 31 x 112cm (12 x 44in) orange fabric
C 112 x 112cm (44 x 44in) main fabric
112 x 140cm (44 x 55in) backing fabric
40 x 112cm (16 x 44in) binding fabric
110 x 150cm (43 x 59in) wadding

SKILLS
Chevron band (see p.101)

SEAM ALLOWANCE
6mm (¼in) throughout, unless otherwise stated

▶▶ PATTERN

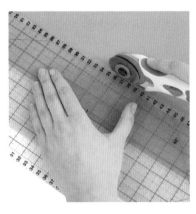

1 Cut 10 strips of fabric each 6.5 x 112cm (2½ x 44in); six from fabric A and four from fabric B.

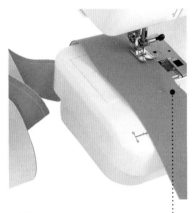

2 Pin, then sew, the first two strips – one of fabric A and one of fabric B – together along the long edges. Repeat to attach five strips together, alternating so you have A, B, A, B, and A. Sew in opposite directions when attaching each strip, to help prevent distortion (see p.60).

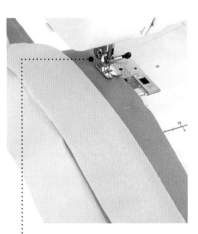

3 Repeat, sewing the remaining five strips together to create a second pieced strip.

4 Iron the finished pieced strips pressing the seam allowances towards the darker fabric.

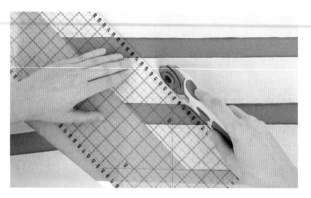

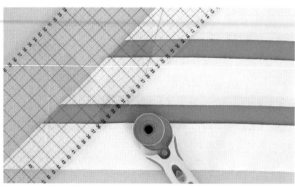

5 Cut the first pieced strip into 6.5cm (2½in) segments on a 45-degree angle. Cut until the entire strip has been cut (see p.101, Step 2).

6 Cut the second pieced strip in the same way, but changing the direction of the angle to the opposite way (see p.101, Step 3).

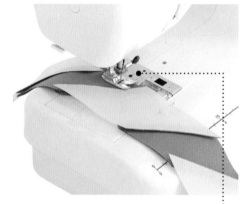

7 Lay out 19 cut pieces, alternating one from each directional group, to create the chevron pattern.

8 Pin and sew the pieces together in pairs. Then, pin and sew the pairs and extra piece together to create one long strip.

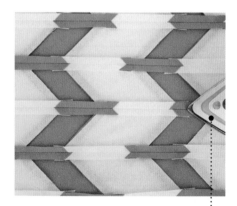

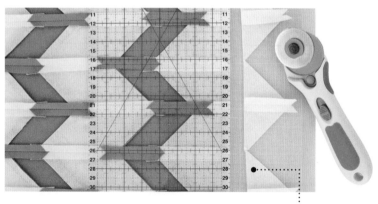

9 Press the seams open at the back of the pieced chevron strip.

10 Trim off the pointed edges of the chevron strip to even both edges (see p.101, Step 5). Make sure to trim each edge the same amount, so that the chevron design is centred in the strip.

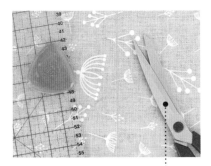

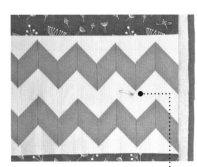

11 Cut the two pieces of front fabric from the main fabric – one 100 x 74cm (39 x 29in) piece for the top and one 100 x 35.5cm (39 x 14in) piece for the bottom.

12 Pin and sew one long edge of the chevron strip right sides together with the bottom edge of the top main fabric piece. Then, pin and sew the other long edge of the chevron strip to the top edge of the bottom main fabric piece to create the quilt top. Press the seams towards the main fabric.

13 Lay out the backing fabric right side down, then the wadding, and then the quilt top right side up. Smooth all of the layers, then pin or tack them together to create the quilt sandwich (see p.44).

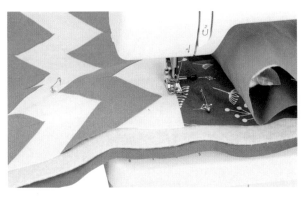

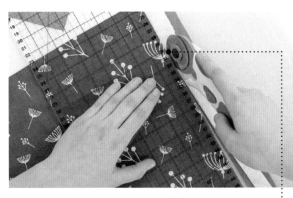

14 Quilt the quilt sandwich using the quilting method and pattern of your choice (see pp.132–133, 134–137).

15 Trim the wadding and backing fabric even with the quilt top, squaring up all of the edges.

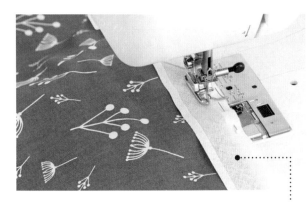

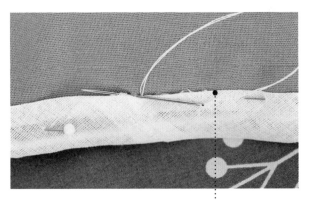

16 Create a 6cm (2½in) wide binding strip from the binding fabric (see pp.46–47) and attach the binding using the double-fold binding method (see p.51), or the method of your choice (see pp.48–51).

17 Finish the binding at the back by hand, slip stitching it in place with a needle and thread.

APPLIQUÉ ZIP POUCH

This bag is so quick and easy that once you've mastered how to make one, you'll want to make many more, and in all shapes and sizes. Use a cotton fabric so that it can easily be thrown in the wash. These bags also make fantastic gifts.

DIFFICULTY LEVEL
Easy

SIZE
22 x 19.5 x 8cm (8⅝ x 7½ x 3⅛in)

TOOLS AND MATERIALS
Quilter's ruler
Rotary cutter
Cutting mat
Pencil
Tracing paper
Scissors
Pins
Sewing machine
Thread to match main fabric
Iron and ironing board
1 standard zip 30cm (12in) long
   (minimum) in a colour to match
   the main fabric
Thin ribbon to match (optional)

FABRICS
54 x 28cm (21¼ x 11in) cotton
   main fabric, plus 12.5 x 12.5cm
   (5 x 5in) extra
54 x 28cm (21¼ x 11in) cotton
   lining fabric
A scrap of fabric with a motif, maximum
   of 10cm (4in) square, that you'd like to
   feature on the front of the make-up bag

SKILLS
Turned reverse appliqué (see pp.124–125)

SEAM ALLOWANCE
6mm (¼in) throughout, unless
   otherwise stated

⟫ PATTERN

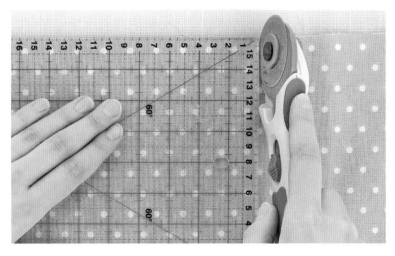

1 Cut two pieces of main fabric and two pieces of lining fabric each 27 x 28cm (10⅝ x 11in).

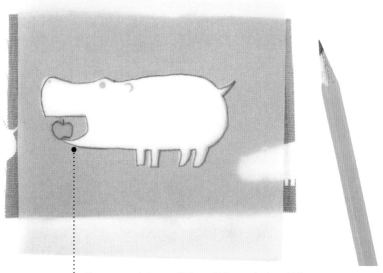

2 Trace around the motif that will feature in the middle of your reverse appliqué to create a template for it.

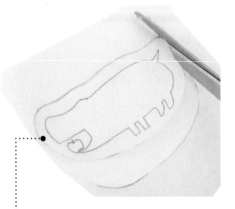

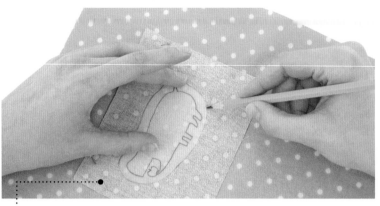

3 Add 1cm (⅜in) extra all around the shape, then cut out the template along this line.

4 Pin the extra 12.5 x 12.5cm (5 x 5in) square of main fabric right sides together onto the front piece of the main fabric so that the top of the rectangle sits about 5cm (2in) down from the top edge of the front fabric. Centre the template in the square and trace around it. This is where your motif will appear on the bag front.

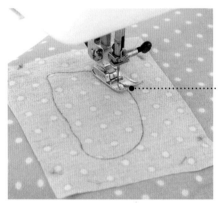

5 Using a matching thread, carefully sew along the traced line.

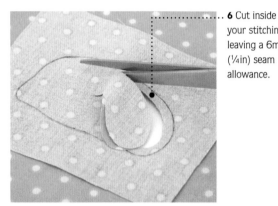

6 Cut inside your stitching, leaving a 6mm (¼in) seam allowance.

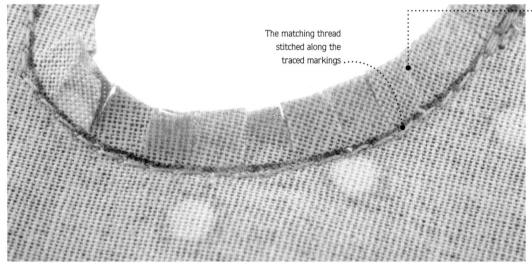

The matching thread stitched along the traced markings

7 Snip into the seam allowance, being careful not to cut any of the stitches (see p.124).

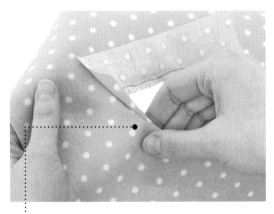

8 Turn the small square of fabric through the hole, to the wrong side of the main front fabric. The wrong side of the square will sit wrong side to the bag front leaving a finished turned-edge seam.

9 Ensure that the shape of the hole forms the same shape as your paper template. Press the seam flat on both sides.

10 Centre the motif under the hole with both fabrics right side up. Pin around the edges leaving enough room to topstitch.

11 Thread your machine with a thread to match your main fabric, then topstitch around the edge of the hole approximately 3mm (⅛in) from the edge using a straight stitch, or a decorative stitch, if you choose to. Remove the pins as you work.

12 Turn the bag front over, then trim the excess fabric from around the motif and the turned-through square to 6mm (¼in). Be careful not to cut the main fabric of the bag front.

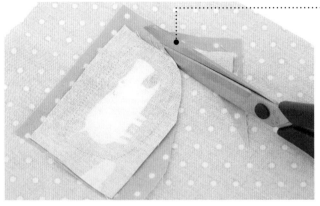

Pin the lining, zip,
and front together,
aligning all three . . . .

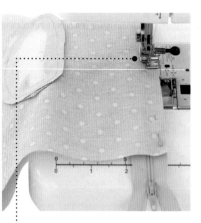

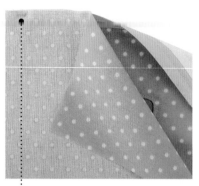

13 Lay a piece of the lining fabric right side up, then lay the zip right side up aligning the top edge with the top edge of the lining. Lay the bag front wrong side up on top of this, aligning the top edge with the top edges of the zip and lining. Pin through all three.

14 Put a zip foot on your machine and stitch through all three layers. Fold the front and lining down on either side of the zip so they both face right side out.

15 Lay the second lining piece right side up, then lay the free edge of the zip – right side up – to align with the top of the lining fabric, then lay the main back fabric right side down on top. Pin through all three layers aligning the edges as in Step 13.

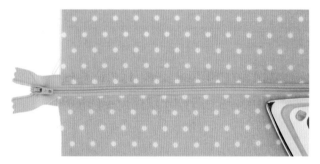

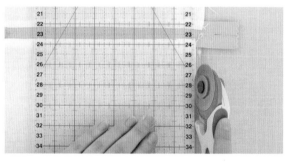

16 Stitch along the edge to attach the zip. Fold the back and back lining down so that the zip is visible between the front and back bags on both the main and lining fabrics. Press as shown. Topstitch at this point if you want. Open up the zip by a few centimeters (inches) so that the pull sits within the main fabric.

17 Using a long quilter's ruler and a rotary cutter and cutting mat, trim all the edges and the ends of the zip even with one another so that the entire width is 23cm (9in). Make sure all the layers are flat and straight before cutting. Trim the bottom edges of the bag front and back so that they sit 24cm (9½in) away from the zip.

18 Fold the bag in half at the zip so the front and back of the main fabrics sit right sides together. Align all the edges and pin around the three raw edges, through all four layers. Leave the zip open.

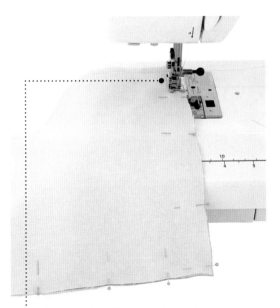

19 Sew around the three pinned raw edges using a 6mm (¼in) seam allowance. Remove the pins as you sew.

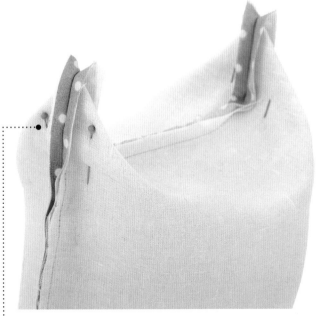

20 Press the seam open. Take the two bottom corners of the bag and pinch them in as shown, so that the bottom seam of the bag aligns with the corresponding side seam on the bag. This will create the boxed corners. Pin either side of the matched seam.

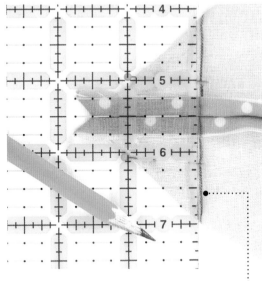

21 Mark a line 3.8cm (1½in) from each corner of the bag, perpendicular to the seams.

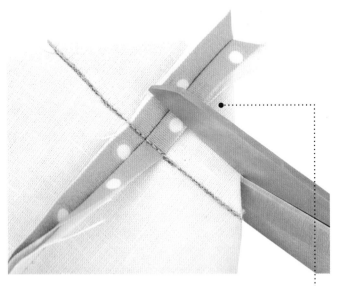

22 Sew along the marked lines, then trim the corner off leaving a 6mm (¼in) seam allowance. Zigzag stitch back and forth over the raw edges to prevent them from fraying and to extend the life of your bag. Carefully turn the bag right side out and press all the seams flat. Thread a matching ribbon through the eye of the zip pull to add an extra touch to the bag.

HAND-QUILTED CUSHION

Hand quilting uses running stitch to hold the layers of the piece together. This lovely cushion cover with a slit opening at the back gives you a chance to try out this simple technique. The finished cover has authentic handmade charm.

DIFFICULTY LEVEL
Easy

SIZE
40 x 40cm (16 x 16in)

TOOLS AND MATERIALS
Rotary cutter
Scissors
Cutting mat
Quilter's ruler
Pins
Safety pins
Large-eyed needle
Threads to match your fabrics
Contrasting embroidery thread
Sewing machine
Iron and ironing board
40cm (16in) square cushion pad

FABRICS
43 x 43cm (17 x 17in) patterned
    front fabric
88 x 52cm (35 x 20½in) backing fabric
45 x 45cm (17¾ x 17¾in) wadding

SKILLS
Hand quilting (see pp.132–133)

SEAM ALLOWANCE
1cm (⅜in) seam allowance throughout,
    unless otherwise stated

TIP
If you find it easier, use tailor's chalk and
    a ruler to draw stitching guidelines, or
    use masking tape to mark straight lines.

▶▶ PATTERN

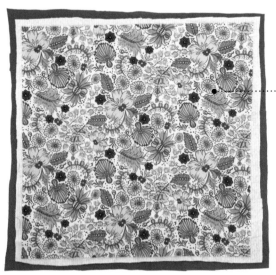

1 For the cushion front, lay a 46 x 46cm (18 x 18in) square of backing fabric on a flat surface. Centre the wadding on top of the backing fabric, then centre the patterned front fabric on top of that.

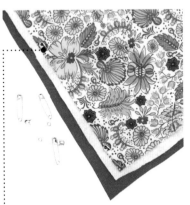

2 Starting from the centre and working outwards, pin the backing, wadding, and front fabric together using safety pins. Make sure that all the layers lie flat and check that the underside of the backing fabric also lies flat (see p.44).

3 Starting at one corner and using a large-eyed needle and a length of embroidery thread, use stab stitch (see p.133) to sew a line through all three layers of fabric. Make the stitches and the gap between them about 6mm (¼in) long. At the opposite edge, tie the thread off at the back.

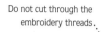
Do not cut through the
embroidery threads

4 Continue sewing rows of running stitch, spacing the rows approximately 1cm (⅜in) apart. Try to keep the stitches and the gaps in line from row to row, as above. Continue until you have stitched the entire top. Remove the safety pins as you work.

5 Use your quilter's ruler and rotary cutter to cut around all four edges to remove the excess wadding and backing fabric, trimming the cushion front to a 42cm (16½in) square.

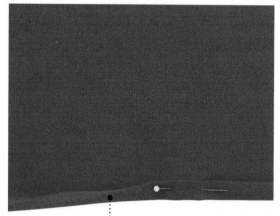

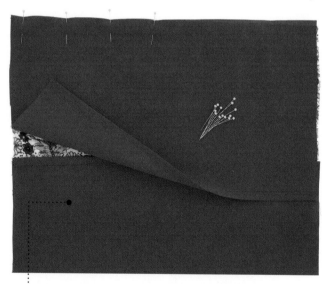

6 To make the cushion back, cut two pieces of backing fabric, each 42 x 26cm (16½ x 10in). Fold one of the long edges of one piece to the wrong side of the fabric by 1cm (⅜in). Fold it again by the same amount to create a neat hem and to enclose the raw edge. Pin the hem in place, check that it is straight, then sew along the edge of the second fold to secure the hem. Repeat on the other piece of fabric.

7 Lay the quilted cushion front right side up. Place one of the back pieces on top, right side down, aligning its long, unhemmed edge with the top raw edge of the cushion front. Place the second back piece right side down on top of the first, aligning its long, unhemmed edge with the bottom raw edge of the cushion front. The two back pieces should overlap. Pin along all four edges.

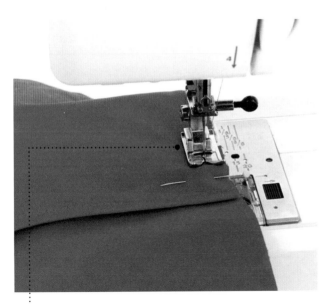

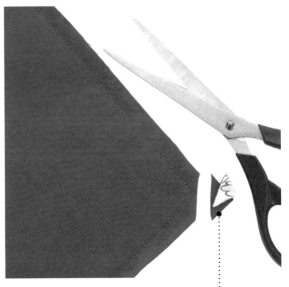

8 Leaving a 1cm (⅜in) seam allowance, sew around all four edges of the cushion cover to secure the back pieces to the cushion front. Forward and reverse stitch over the overlapped edges. Remove the pins as you work.

9 Snip off all four corners, taking care not to cut through the stitches. Turn the cushion cover to the right side through the opening in the back. Iron, then insert the cushion pad.

Loose, casual running stitches give this cushion its handmade charm. To add even more colour and to give the cushion a very personalized touch, try using more than one colour of embroidery thread, changing colour after every few rows.

QUILTED POT HOLDERS

These pot holders are quick to whip up in any size. Each pot holder is like a mini-quilt with a backing, wadding, and front all quilted together and bound.

They're the perfect project for trying out your quilting skills, or for using up scraps of fabric.

DIFFICULTY LEVEL
Easy

SIZE
19cm (7½in) square

TOOLS AND MATERIALS
Quilter's ruler
Cutting mat
Rotary cutter
Sewing machine
Pins
Threads to match the fabrics and binding tapes

FABRICS
21.5 x 43cm (8½ x 17in) main, patterned cotton fabric
21.5 x 43cm (8½ x 17in) insulated wadding
21.5 x 43cm (8½ x 17in) cotton towelling fabric
100cm (39in) bias binding tape

SKILLS
Machine quilting (see pp.134–137)
Binding with pre-made bias binding (see pp.48–49)

SEAM ALLOWANCE
6mm (¼in) throughout, unless otherwise stated

▶▶ PATTERN

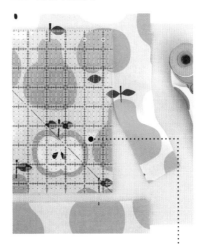

1 Cut one piece of main fabric, one piece of insulated wadding, and once piece of towelling fabric all 21.5cm (8½in) square. Then, cut one piece of main fabric, one piece of towelling fabric, and one piece of insulated wadding all 16.5 x 21.5cm (6½ x 8½in).

2 Pin each piece of main fabric wrong sides together with its corresponding piece of towelling, placing the insulated wadding in the middle. Place the pins inside the motif to be quilted so that they will not be in the way of your stitching lines.

3 Using a matching or complementary thread in the top of your machine and a thread to match your towelling in your bobbin, stitch around each shape on both pinned units. Alternatively, you can quilt the units using the pattern of your choice.

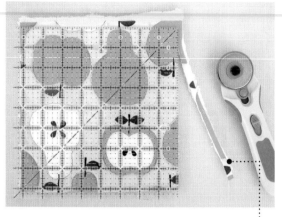

ZIGZAG THE EDGES

4 Once you are done quilting both pieces, trim the larger unit an equal amount on all four sides so that it is 19cm (7½in) square. Trim the smaller unit so that it is 19 x 14cm (7½ x 5½in).

5 Zigzag stitch around all four raw edges of both units to keep the edges neat and tidy.

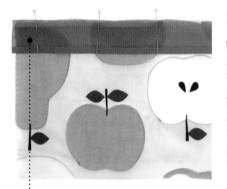

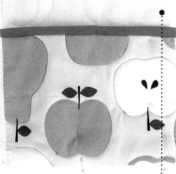

6 Cut a piece of bias binding 19cm (7½in) long. Open it up and pin it along the top edge of the smaller unit. Sew it in place, then fold it around to the back and stitch it in place either by machine or by hand (see pp.48–49).

7 Lay the large unit towelling side up, then lay the smaller unit on top of it, towelling side down. Align the bottom and side edges, pinning in place. Stitch the two units together, around the three unfinished edges of the small unit, leaving a 6mm (¼in) seam allowance to create the pot holder.

8 Attach a piece of bias binding to fit all the way around the pot holder, mitring the corners and finishing by hand or machine (see pp.48–49).

POT HOLDER VARIATION

You can easily make variations on the pocket-style pot holder just shown. If you'd like to make one without a pocket and with fabric on both sides, cut two squares of main fabric and one square of insulated wadding of the same size. Sandwich the wadding between the two layers of fabric, pin, and quilt as you wish. Bind all four edges.

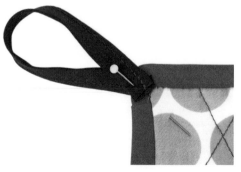

You can attach a handy loop to your pot holders if you'd like to be able to hang them. Fold a piece of binding tape approximately 15.5cm (6in) in half, along the length, wrong sides together. Fold in the two raw ends so that they will not be visible. Stitch along the edges to create a long thin strip. Create a loop out of the strip, as shown right, and pin it to the corner of the potholder. Stitch it securely in place.

KANTHA STITCH THROW

Made from snuggly flannel, this throw is perfect for chilly evenings. You can design and stitch any pattern you wish. Here we've quilted a geometric pattern with borders around it. Be sure to mark the whole design before you begin sewing.

DIFFICULTY LEVEL
Easy

SIZE
118 x 163cm (46½ x 64in)

TOOLS AND MATERIALS
Scissors
Curved safety pins
Card
Pencil
Spray bottle or sponge
Rotary cutter
Cutting mat
Quilter's ruler
Water-soluble pen
Roll of 2.5cm (1in) masking tape
Large-eyed needle
Five different-coloured embroidery,
   or quilting, threads
Sewing machine (optional)
Thread to match the main fabric
Sewing needle

FABRIC
200 x 275cm (78 x 108in) of flannel for
   the main fabric front, back, and binding
123 x 165cm (48 x 65in) wadding

SKILLS
Hand quilting (see pp.132–133)

SEAM ALLOWANCE
Hand quilt following the pattern

▶▶ PATTERN

MAKE THE QUILT SANDWICH
Cut two pieces of main fabric both 120 x 165cm (47 x 65in). Lay one piece right side down, then lay the wadding to fit on top of it. Lay the other main fabric piece right side up on top so all the edges are even. Smooth all the layers from the centre outwards and once smooth, use curved safety pins to pin the layers together (see p.44).

MARK THE DESIGN
Measure and mark the centre of the quilt sandwich. Using the templates on page 214 and a water-soluble pen, mark the pattern on the front of the quilt sandwich. Use the masking tape to mark the borders and your quilter's ruler to make sure everything is sitting even and square with one another. If you are unhappy with the design at any point, use water to remove the pen and begin again.

QUILT THE PATTERN
Working from the centre outwards and readjusting the safety pins as needed, begin to quilt the pattern using stab stitch (see p.41) and the colours indicated on the diagram. Bury the knots in the fabric at the back to hide them (see p.132). Cut a piece of embroidery thread long enough to sew each shape. Remove any safety pins that fall within the quilted sections as you work, but leave the pins around the edges. Remove the masking tape when you are done.

ATTACH THE BINDING
Trim the edges of the quilt square with each other and the stitching. Cut and piece together a binding strip 6.5 x 585cm (2½ x 230in), (see pp.46–47). Attach the strip using the double-fold binding method (see p.51).

PATTERN LAYOUT

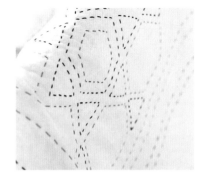

Keep the stitches the same size as you work, so that every shape is uniform in appearance. Bury the knots in the fabric, always at the back of the quilt.

FLYING GEESE QUILT

The instructions for piecing this quilt are fast and simple, leaving no waste. The flying geese blocks are created in pairs. Here, we've kept the pairs together in our final layout, but you may wish to separate the pairs throughout the quilt top.

DIFFICULTY LEVEL
Medium

SIZE
100 x 115cm (39 x 45in)

TOOLS AND MATERIALS
Measuring tape
Quilter's ruler
Rotary cutter
Cutting mat
Scissors
Sewing machine
Threads to match your fabrics
Iron and ironing board
Safety pins
Quilting thread

FABRICS
A 80 x 112cm (32 x 44in) dark fabric for the geese, or three fat quarters
B 80 x 112cm (32 x 44in) light fabric, or five fat eighths, for the backgrounds
C 20 x 112cm (8 x 44in) fabric for the narrow inner border
D 60 x 112cm (23½ x 44in) fabric for the wide outer border
50 x 112cm (20 x 44in) fabric for 1.2cm (½in) double fold binding
130 x 112cm (51 x 44in) backing fabric
115 x 130cm (46 x 51in) wadding

SKILLS
Flying geese (see p.67)

SEAM ALLOWANCE
6mm (¼in) throughout

▶ PATTERN

CUT THE FABRICS
Cut 21 square pieces from fabric A, each measuring 16cm (6¼in). Cut 84 square pieces from fabric B, each measuring 9.5cm (3⅜in). Cut four strips from fabric C, selvedge to selvedge, each measuring 4cm (1½in). Cut four strips from fabric D, selvedge to selvedge, each measuring 12cm (5in).

MAKE THE BLOCKS
Lightly draw a diagonal line across the squares from fabric B (see Chart 1, overleaf). Place two of these squares on a square from fabric A, right sides together and on diagonally opposite corners. The fabric B squares will overlap slightly in the middle (see Chart 2, overleaf). Stitch a 6mm (¼in) seam on either side of the drawn lines (see Chart 3, overleaf). Cut along the drawn line and press the pieces open (see Charts 4 and 5, overleaf). Place another square from fabric B on the corner of the stitched piece (see Chart 6, overleaf). Stitch a 6mm (¼in) seam on either side of the drawn line (see Chart 7, overleaf). Cut along the drawn line and press open the pieces (see Chart 8, overleaf). This completes the block (see Chart 9, overleaf). Repeat with the remaining squares from fabric A and B until you have 84 blocks, each measuring 14.6 x 7.5cm (5¾ x 3in).

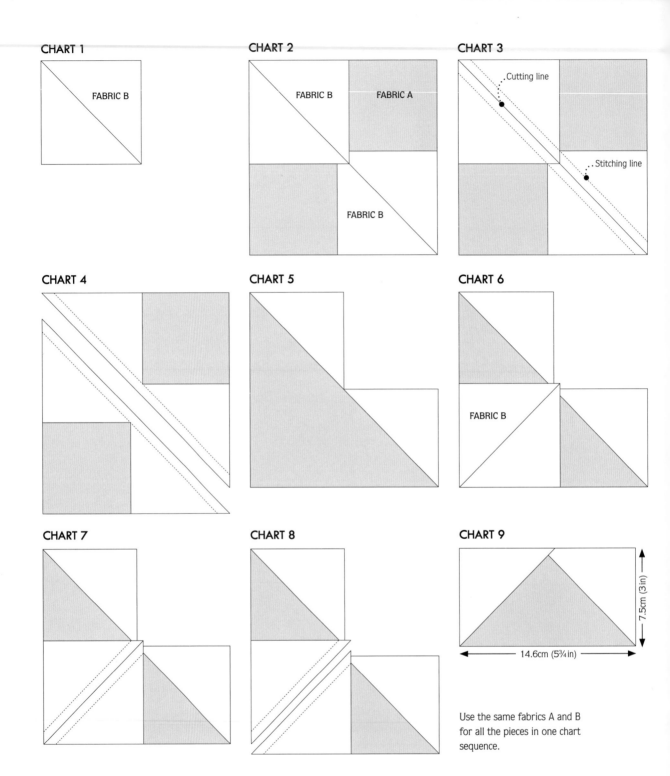

CHART 1

FABRIC B

CHART 2

FABRIC B

FABRIC A

FABRIC B

CHART 3

Cutting line

Stitching line

CHART 4

CHART 5

CHART 6

FABRIC B

CHART 7

CHART 8

CHART 9

7.5cm (3in)

14.6cm (5¾in)

Use the same fabrics A and B for all the pieces in one chart sequence.

SEW THE QUILT TOP

Lay the blocks out in 14 rows, in the pattern of your choice, with six blocks in each row. Sew the blocks in each row together. Sew the rows together, matching the corners of the flying geese blocks (see pp.62–63).

Stitch the narrow border to both the left and right sides of the quilt top, squaring off the excess border strips. Then, attach the border to the top and bottom of the quilt. Stitch the larger outer border in the same left, right, top, and bottom sequence.

ASSEMBLE THE LAYERS

Lay the backing fabric on a flat surface, right side down. Carefully lay the wadding on top. Smooth out the two to make sure there are no folds. Then lay the quilt top on the wadding. The wadding and the backing fabric will overhang the quilt top by a few centimetres (inches) each. Starting from the centre and working outwards, pin the layers together using safety pins, making sure all the layers sit flat and even with one another. Check the back of the quilt as well.

Machine or hand quilt with the design of your choice.

ATTACH THE BINDING

Lay the quilt, right side up, on a flat surface. Follow the instructions for double-fold binding, as shown on page 51, or bind the quilt using the method of your choice.

Using a variegated quilting thread makes more of a feature of the quilting stitches. You can use a quilting thread that either blends in, or stands out, depending on your personal preference.

TEMPLATES

SIMPLE SQUARES TOTE (pp.154–159)
Enlarge by 200% on a photocopier

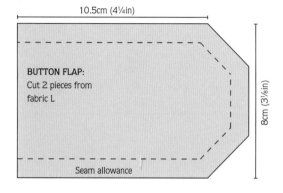

10.5cm (4¼in)

BUTTON FLAP:
Cut 2 pieces from
fabric L

8cm (3⅛in)

Seam allowance

– – – – Stitching line

DIAMOND COASTERS/LAVENDER BAG (pp.168–171)
Enlarge by 200% on a photocopier

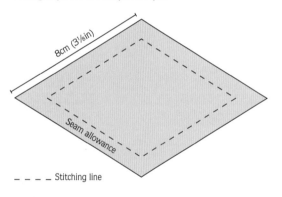

8cm (3⅛in)

Seam allowance

– – – – Stitching line

ELECTRONIC DEVICE COVER (pp.182–185)
Actual size

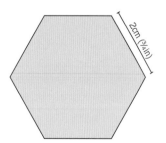

2cm (¾in)

TRIANGLE FLOOR CUSHION (pp.160–167)
Enlarge by 200% on a photocopier

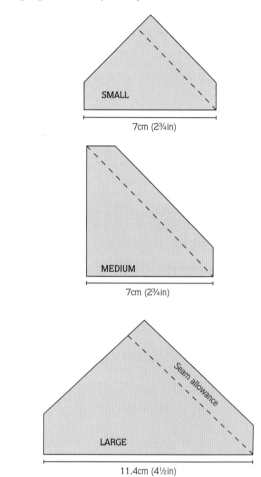

SMALL

7cm (2¾in)

MEDIUM

7cm (2¾in)

LARGE

Seam allowance

11.4cm (4½in)

– – – – Stitching line

KANTHA STITCH THROW (pp.208–209)
Enlarge by 400% on a photocopier

5cm (2in)

Triangle

Large hexagon

6cm (2½in)

Small hexagon
4cm (1½in)

DRESDEN PLATE CUSHION (pp.176–181)

Use the measurements in the diagrams below to make the templates

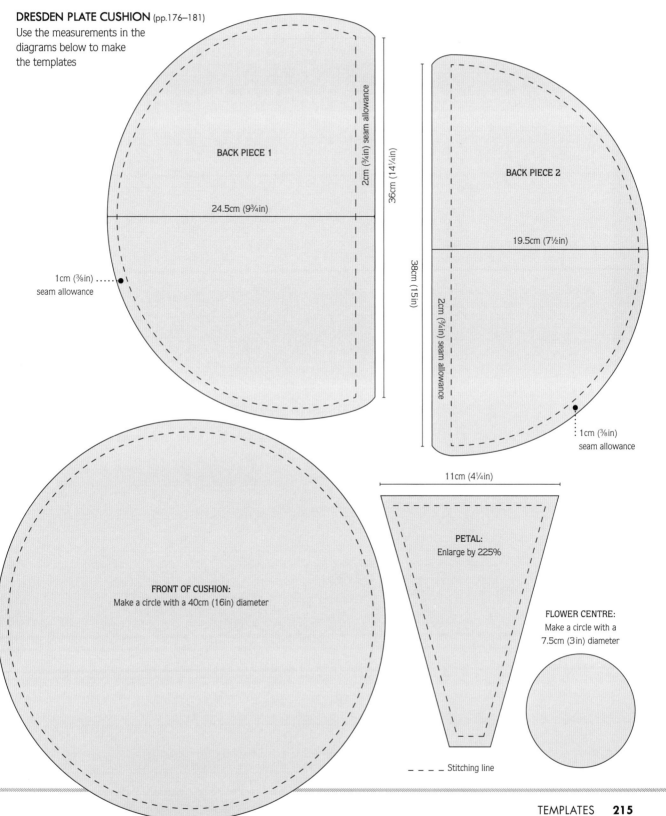

BACK PIECE 1

2cm (¾in) seam allowance

36cm (14¼in)

24.5cm (9¾in)

1cm (⅜in) ..... seam allowance

BACK PIECE 2

19.5cm (7½in)

38cm (15in)

2cm (¾in) seam allowance

1cm (⅜in) seam allowance

PETAL:
Enlarge by 225%

11cm (4¼in)

FRONT OF CUSHION:
Make a circle with a 40cm (16in) diameter

FLOWER CENTRE:
Make a circle with a
7.5cm (3in) diameter

– – – Stitching line

GLOSSARY

Appliqué
From the French verb *appliquer,* meaning "to apply", a decorative technique in which shapes are cut from one fabric and applied to another, either by stitching them in place or by heat bonding with fusible bonding web.

Backstitch
A hand stitch used to seam patchwork. A more secure alternative to running stitch.

Bagging out
A finishing technique that involves placing the quilt top and backing right sides together, on top of the wadding, and then stitching around the edges before turning the quilt through to the right side – thereby obviating the need for a separate binding.

Bias
The diagonal grain of a woven fabric, at 45-degrees to the straight grain.

Binding
A narrow strip of fabric used to cover the raw edges of a quilt to provide a neat finish and prevent it from fraying. For straight edges, the binding can be cut on the straight grain; bias-cut binding has more stretch, and should always be used for curved edges.

Blanket stitch
Decorative hand or machine stitch worked along the raw or finished edge of fabric to neaten it. Often used in appliqué work.

Block
A single design unit in patchwork and appliqué. Patchwork blocks traditionally fall into one of four main categories: four-patch (two rows of two patches), nine-patch (three rows of three patches), five-patch (five rows of five patches), and seven-patch (seven rows of seven patches).

Bodkin
A large needle with a ball-point end and a large eye. Most commonly used for threading elastic or ribbon through a tube or casing, but it can also be used for turning thin tubes of fabric right side out.

Buttonhole
Opening through which a button is inserted to form a fastening. Buttonholes are usually machine stitched but may also be worked by hand or piped for reinforcement or decorative effect.

Buttonhole stitch
A hand stitch that wraps over the raw edges of a buttonhole to neaten and strengthen it. Machine-stitched buttonholes are worked with a special close zigzag stitch.

Chain piecing
A method of piecing together patchwork units by feeding them through the sewing machine in sequence without lifting the presser foot or breaking the thread so that they form a chain with a short length of thread between each one.

Dye magnet
An untreated piece of plain, colourless fabric used to attract loose dye from other fabrics during a wash-cycle to prevent them from bleeding into other fabrics and ruining the colours. Dye magnets are available commercially, but you can also use a piece of untreated, white towelling. Also known as colour catchers.

Dog ears
The pieces of a seam allowance that stick out past the edges of the fabric when two pieces of fabric are sewn together on an angle.

English paper piecing
A traditional patchwork method for making a quilt of mosaic shapes by tacking the fabric pieces (all of which have some bias edges) to pre-cut paper templates the size of the finished element.

Facing
A separate layer of fabric placed on the inside of an edge of fabric to finish off raw edges. A useful way to finish off shaped bindings such as scallops.

Feed dogs
The thin, short metal bars in the needle plate of the sewing machine, which move back and forth as you sew, pulling the fabric forward at an even speed.

Finger pressing
Pressing a seam using your thumbnail. It is usually used as a temporary solution for seams within a larger piece of patchwork that will be pressed with an iron at a later stage. Take care not to distort the fabric.

Foundation piecing
A patchwork technique in which fabric pieces, or patches, are stitched to a foundation, either a lightweight fabric such as calico, or to paper which is removed once the design is completed.

Fusible bonding web
A non-woven material impregnated with heat-activated adhesive. Widely used in machine appliqué work.

Fussy cutting
Isolating an individual motif on a printed fabric and cutting it out to use as a feature in a patchwork or appliqué block.

Grading a seam
Trimming back one of the two pieces of seam allowances in a seam, after sewing, to help a seam sit smoothly when pressed to one side.

Grain
Lengthways and crossways direction of threads in a fabric. Fabric grain effects how a fabric drapes.

Hem
The edge of a piece of fabric neatened and stitched to prevent unravelling. There are several ways to hem an edge, but the most common way in soft furnishings is to fold the raw edge of the fabric over twice, then stitch along the fold, closing the raw edge inside.

Inferfacing
A fabric placed on the wrong side of another fabric to give it structure and support. Available in different thicknesses, interfacing can be fusible (bonds to the fabric when heat is applied) or non-fusible (needs to be sewn to the fabric).

Lining
Underlaying fabric used to give a neat finish to an item.

Medallion
A style of quilt in which a large central motif is surrounded by several borders.

Mirrorwork
Also called shisha work, a traditional form of textile decoration from Central Asia and India that involves stitching around or over small discs of mirror, glass, or tin to hold them in place on the fabric.

Mitre
To finish a corner by stitching adjacent sides of fabric together at a 45-degree angle. Or, the diagonal line made where two edges of a piece of fabric meet at a corner, produced by folding.

Muslin
Fine, plain, open-weave cotton.

Nap
The raised pile of fabric made during the weaving process, or a print on a fabric which runs one way. When cutting out pattern pieces, ensure the nap runs in the same direction.

Overcasting
Also known as whipstitch, this is a hand stitch used particularly in English paper piecing.

Patch
An individual piece of fabric used in making a patchwork design. Patches may be whole squares or rectangles, or subdivided into triangle units, curved units, or combinations thereof.

Patchwork
The technique of stitching together small pieces of fabric to make a larger one.

Pile
Raised loops on the surface of a fabric, for example, velvet.

Plain-weave fabric
A tightly woven fabric in which the warp and weft form a simple criss-cross pattern. The number of threads in each direction are not necessarily equal. Examples of plain-weave fabrics include cotton, linen, and silk.

Presser foot
The part of a sewing machine that is lowered on to the fabric to hold it in place over the needle plate while stitching. There are many different types of feet available.

Quilting
The process of stitching the three layers of a quilt (top, wadding, and backing) together. In addition to serving a practical purpose in holding the three layers together, the quilting stitch pattern often forms an integral part of the quilt design. It is normally marked out on the quilt top in advance and may consist of a geometric grid of squares or diamond shapes, concentric lines that echo shapes within the design, intricate shapes such as hearts, feathers, and swags, or a continuous meandering pattern.

Quilting guide
Also known as a quilting bar. An I-shaped metal bar which attaches to the back of the presser foot and allows a quilter to stitch evenly spaced lines by following the previous line of quilting stitches. The bar can be adjusted to different widths.

Quilt sandwich
The three layers of a quilt: the top, wadding, and backing. The quilt top and backing form the "bread" of the sandwich and the wadding forms the filling.

Raw edge
Any cut edge of fabric. Raw edges are usually hidden in seams or turned under and hemmed or stitched in place, as in appliqué. Some techniques depend for their effect on leaving the raw edge unstitched.

Reef knot
A type of double knot which is made symmetrically by tieing a single knot with right over left, then a second single knot with left over right, or vice versa. Also known as a square knot.

Registration marks
The marks on a sewing pattern that should be transferred to the fabric when cutting out. They are often in the form of notches, with the notches on one pattern piece corresponding to the notches on other pattern pieces, acting as a guide for matching, pinning, and sewing two pattern pieces together accurately.

Reverse stitch
Machine stitch that stitches backwards over a row of stitches to secure the threads.

Right side
The front of a piece of fabric, the side that will normally be in view when the piece is assembled.

Rocking stitch
The ideal stitch for hand quilting in which the needle takes several stitches up and down vertically before pulling the thread through.

Running stitch
A simple, evenly spaced, straight hand stitch separated by equal-sized spaces, used for seaming and gathering.

Sashing
Strips of fabric interspersed between blocks when making a quilt top.

Seam
The join formed when two pieces of fabric are sewn together.

Seam allowance
The amount of fabric allowed for on a pattern where sections are to be joined together by a seam. The standard seam allowance in patchwork is 6mm (¼in).

Seam edge
The cut edge of a seam allowance.

Seamline
The line along which a seam should be stitched.

Seam ripper
A small, pointed, hooked tool with a blade on the inside edge of the hook used for undoing seams and unpicking stitches.

Seam roller
Tubular pressing aid for pressing seams open on fabrics that mark.

Selvedge
The rigid edge woven into each side of a length of fabric to prevent the fabric from fraying or unravelling. It occurs when the weft thread turns at the edge of the warp threads to start the next row.

Set or setting
The way the blocks that make up a quilt top are arranged. Blocks may be straight set (stitched together edge to edge, with each block oriented the same way), or set "on point" (turned on the diagonal so that they appear as diamonds rather than squares). Pieced and appliqué blocks may be alternated with plain "spacer" blocks, or blocks may be rotated to create secondary patterns.

Setting in
In patchwork, sewing one shape or patch into an acute angle formed when two other shapes have been joined together.

Sewing gauge
Measuring tool with an adjustable slider for checking small measurements, such as hem depths and seam allowance.

Slip stitch
A hidden stitch used mainly in appliqué work.

Stab stitch
An alternative hand quilting stitch used particularly on thicker fabric layers. The needle is taken up then down to make individual stitches.

Stitch in the ditch
A line of straight stitches sewn on the right side of the work, in the ditch created by a seam. Used as a form of hidden quilting.

Straight grain
The parallel threads of a woven fabric running at 90 degrees to either the lengthways (warp) or crossways (weft) direction of the weave.

Straight stitch
Plain machine stitch, used for most applications. The length of the stitch can be altered to suit the fabric.

String piecing
In patchwork, similar to strip piecing, but the strips can be of uneven width.

Strip piecing
A patchwork technique in which long strips of fabric are sewn together and then cut apart before being reassembled in a different sequence. The method is used to create many popular blocks, including log cabin and Seminole patchwork.

Tacking
A temporary stitch used to hold pieces of fabric together or for transferring pattern markings to fabric. It can be worked by hand or machine and can be a straight line or individual doubled stitches.

Tailor's chalk
Square- or triangular-shaped pieces of chalk used to mark fabric. Available in a variety of colours, tailor's chalk can be removed easily by brushing.

Tension
The tautness of the stitching in a seam.

Thimble
A metal or plastic cap that fits over the top of a finger to protect it when hand sewing.

Throat
The space on a sewing machine underneath the arm. Standard sewing machines have a throat space of less than 30cm (12in). When working on many quilts the project will have to be rolled or folded so that it fits within the throat, neatly out of the way of the needle.

Topstitch
Machine straight stitching worked on the right side of an item, close to the finished edge, for decorative effect. Sometimes stitched in a contrasting colour.

Topstitched seam
A seam finished with a row of topstitching for decorative effect on soft furnishings and garments.

Tying
A utilitarian quilting method in which thread, string, cord, etc., is stitched through the layers and tied in a secure knot.

Wadding
Also called batting, this is a layer of filling made from polyester, cotton, wool, or even silk and used to provide warmth and give body to a quilt. Wadding is available in many different lofts, or thicknesses.

Warp
The vertical threads of a woven fabric, also known as the lengthways grain.

Weft
The horizontal threads of a woven fabric, also known as the crossways grain.

Wrong side
The reverse of a piece of fabric, the side that will normally be hidden from view when the piece is made up.

Yo-yo
A type of patchwork made from a round piece of fabric that has been gathered. Usually, many yo-yos are joined together, but they can also be individually applied within larger patchwork pieces to add decoration.

Zigzag stitch
A machine stitch used to neaten and secure seam edges and for decorative purposes. The width and length of the zigzag can be altered.

Zip foot
Narrow machine foot with a single toe that can be positioned on either side of the needle.

INDEX

CONTRIBUTORS

BETH BLIGHT

Beth studied a degree in performance design at Central St Martins University in London, UK, graduating in 2013. She has a strong interest in making costumes for theatre, but loves sewing for the home and making cushions, quilts, and writing craft project instructions. Beth made the Dresden plate cushion (see pp.176–181).
bettyblight.wordpress.com

CHERYL OWEN

Cheryl is an innovative and experienced crafter. Having originally trained and worked in the fashion industry, Cheryl went on to apply her design and making skills to the fields of craft, especially sewing, paper crafts, and making jewellery. She is the author of more than 40 craft books, designs craft kits, and is a regular contributor of craft features to leading magazines and partworks. Cheryl made the simple squares tote (see pp.154–159) and triangle floor cushion (see pp.160–167).

SABI WESTOBY

Having been a traditional quilter for many years, retirement from full-time work in 2008 led to a change in direction and Sabi now makes art quilts and mixed media works. Combining paper and textile, paint and stitch, collage and appliqué, Sabi creates works inspired by both the natural and human-made worlds. Sabi is excited by the challenge of embracing new techniques and exploring unknown materials, which can be dyed, printed, manipulated, burnt or stitched. She likes to create fabrics in vibrant colours and overprint them with her own designs. Sabi made the flying geese quilt (see pp.210–213).
www.sabiwestoby.com

MICHAEL CAPUTO, CONSULTANT

Michael Caputo was born and raised in New York, US. As a design graduate of the Fashion Institute of Technology in New York City, Michael has been using his skills to design and engineer children's pop-up books since he graduated from university.

Initially taught to quilt by his mother, Michael uses his background in colour theory and layout to create one-of-a-kind quilts. Exploring different methods and techniques, Michael continues to quilt on a daily basis. He taught quilting classes in London for several years and currently lives with his family in Raleigh, North Carolina, US.

ACKNOWLEDGMENTS

For content previously published in *Quilting: Patchwork and Appliqué* (2014).

DK LONDON

Project Editor Kathryn Meeker; **Senior Art Editor** Glenda Fisher; **Editor** Hilary Mandleberg; **Managing Editor** Penny Smith; **Managing Art Editor** Marianne Markham; **Senior Jacket Designer** Nicola Powling; **Producer, Pre-Production** Andy Hilliard; **Senior Producer** Ché Creasey; **Creative Technical Support** Sonia Charbonnier; **Photography** Ruth Jenkinson; **Art Director/Stylist for Photography** Isabel de Cordova; **Art Director** Jane Bull; **Publisher** Mary Ling

DK DELHI

Senior Editor Dorothy Kikon; **Senior Art Editor** Ivy Roy; **Editor** Arani Sinha; **Art Editors** Neha Wahi, Swati Katyal, and Tanya Mehrotra; **Managing Editor** Alicia Ingty; **Managing Art Editor** Navidita Thapa; **Pre-Production Manager** Sunil Sharma; **DTP Designers** Satish Gaur, Anurag Trivedi, and Manish Upreti

Dorling Kindersley would like to thank the following people and companies for their invaluable input, time, and dedication: **proofreader** Angela Baynham; **indexer** Marie Lorimer; **photography assistant** Julie Stewart; **additional photography** Andy Crawford; **design assistance** Charlotte Johnson and Charlotte Bull; **editorial assistance** Laura Palosuo; **original project consultancy** Lucinda Ganderton; **location for photography** 1st Option and jj Locations; **prop hire** Backgrounds and China & Co; **fabric swatches** The Eternal Maker: www.eternalmaker.com, Ray Stitch: www.raystitch.co.uk; **models** Aleyah Ali, Eloise Fenton, Leo Flynn, Martha Jenkinson, Ella Kwan, Emily Nyamayaro, Luka Pavicevic, and Dylan Wightwick All other projects were made by the team at DK.

THIS EDITION

Indexer Vanessa Bird

DK LONDON
Senior Editor Dawn Titmus
Senior Designers Glenda Fisher, Hannah Moore
Managing Editor Ruth O'Rourke
Design Manager Marianne Markham
Senior Production Editor Tony Phipps
Production Controller Kariss Ainsworth
Jacket Designer Amy Cox
Jacket Coordinator Lucy Philpott
Art Director Maxine Pedliham
Publishing Director Katie Cowan

DK DELHI
Editor Arani Sinha
Pre-Production Manager Sunil Sharma
DTP Designers Manish Upreti, Satish Gaur

Material in this publication was first published in Great
Britain in *Quilting: Patchwork and Appliqué*, 2014.
This edition published in 2022
by Dorling Kindersley Limited
One Embassy Gardens, 8 Viaduct Gardens,
London, SW11 7BW

The authorized representative in the EEA is
Dorling Kindersley Verlag GmbH. Arnulfstr. 124,
80636 Munich, Germany

A CIP catalogue record for this book is available from the
British Library.
ISBN: 978-0-2415-3148-8

Printed and bound in China

For the curious

www.dk.com

This book was made with Forest Stewardship
Council ™ certified paper – one small step in
DK's commitment to a sustainable future.

For more information go to www.dk.com/our-green-pledge